Management as Music

Management as Music

Applying the Insights of Music Theory to Leadership

Matt Allen

WESTBRAE LITERARY GROUP

Copyright © 2024 Matt Allen
All rights reserved. No part of this book may be reproduced, distributed, or transmitted in any form or by any means, including photocopying, recording, or other electronic or mechanical methods, without the prior written permission of the author, except in the case of brief quotations embodied in critical reviews and certain other noncommercial uses permitted by copyright law.

ISBN: 979-8-9917199-1-9
Published by Westbrae Literary Group
Berkeley, California
Jon-David Hague, Founding Editor

For more information about this and other titles from Westbrae Literary Group, visit us at westbraeliterarygroup.com or email us at info@westbraeliterarygroup.com

Cover art by James B. Janknegt

Dedicated to those who have inspired me to sing and lead:

Nelda Allen
Sherry Upshaw Christy
Randy Edwards
Joyce English

"I want the power of music--that Spirit--to transform those who perform and those who will hear the message."
--Dr. Anton Armstrong

"Where words fail, music speaks"
--Hans Christian Anderson

"A small thing, but in a dissonant world, every moment of harmony counts--and if we share music, we might just shout in anger a little less and sing in unity more. Or so we can hope." -- Jon Meacham

"Music is a higher revelation than all wisdom and philosophy." -- Ludwig van Beethoven

"When I hear music ... I am related to the earliest times, and to the latest." -- Henry David Thoreau

"Music is not sound. Music is using sound to organize emotions in time." --Krystian Zimerman

"The effect of music is so very much more powerful and penetrating than that of other arts, for these others speak only of the shadow, but music of essence." --Arthur Schopenhauer

"Music has the ability to shape character." --Aristotle

"Music can name the unnameable and communicate the unknowable." --Leonard Bernstein

CONTENTS

Introduction..1

1. The Melodic Imperative and the Power of Story............10
2. The Humility of Harmony...17
3. In Praise of Wurlitzers...27
4. The Secret of Relative Pitch..30
5. Embracing the Beauty of Dissonance...........................36
6. Managing Modulations..40
7. Descants and the Intentionality of Inspiration................49
8. The Pentatonic Scale and the Sanctity of Safe Spaces....52
9. Management in Sonata Form......................................59
10. Startling with Silence...61
11. The Cruciality of Counterpoint..................................65
12. Helen Keller's "Ode to Joy".......................................68
Conclusion..70
Afterword...76
Appendix..79
Notes..101

INTRODUCTION

An Overture: Bending Toward Beauty

When managers search to understand and interpret their distinctive approaches to leadership, they often use metaphor as a theoretical framework. Scores of books, articles, webinars, and podcasts have utilized such diverse metaphors as sports, movies, and warfare to provide a comprehensive strategy for effective leadership.

Metaphor is an attractive managerial technique because it opens the mind to view the world in new and creative dimensions and has "a way of holding the most truth in the least space" (Orson Scott Card).

> *"Metaphor is an attractive technique because it opens the mind to view the world in new and creative dimensions..."*

But unprecedented resignations and low employee morale during the COVID-19 pandemic exposed the current managerial metaphors to be inadequate in meeting the deepest needs of our teams.

In response, some managers abandoned the idea of a comprehensive strategy, opting for a triage approach to leadership. Others threw in the towel altogether, concluding that the modern environment provided little opportunity for professional growth, effectiveness, or fulfillment.

Management as Music

How, then, should we respond to such unprecedented managerial challenges? Is there any attractive alternative? Perhaps mythologist Joseph Campbell had the right idea when he wrote that "(i)f you want to change the world, you have to change the metaphor."

So think with me a moment: What metaphor best captures the richness and complexity of managing others? What metaphor best equips leaders to change the world? What metaphor breaks through the daily noise and chaos of modern life to reach the center of the human heart?

Contemplating the answer to those questions, I remembered the moment I discovered, in my grandparents' attic, a certificate of proficiency that my great grandfather received from Patton's Normal Music School in the late 1800s. Gazing on that faded and discolored paper, I immediately formed a connection--through a mutual love of music--with a relative I had never met. I felt like Thoreau: "When I hear music ... I am related to the earliest times, and to the latest." Is there any other vessel that can transport us back a hundred years in an instant?

Or picture the viral videos of "flash mob" operas that became popular several years ago. These videos showcased professional opera singers spontaneously launching into song amid random, bustling crowds of unsuspecting bystanders. Out of the chaos of individual, clamoring voices

An Overture: Bending Toward Beauty

emerged *music* that was beautiful and utterly transcendent. Is there any other force in the universe that can take the rawness of the human condition and, in a moment, bend it toward beauty?

Or consider the story of Chinese pianist Liu Shih-Kun, who burst on to the classical music scene when he placed second at the 1958 Tchaikovsky Piano Competition. After the Cultural Revolution descended, Shih-Kun was imprisoned for nearly eight years. Sitting isolated in confinement, he combated depression and despair by composing music in his mind--eventually writing a concerto, despite no pen, paper, or piano to assist. In that dusty jail cell, *music* transformed despair into a lifeline of hope.

Or take the moment in December 1987 when famed pianist Van Cliburn was asked to play during a White House summit between American President Ronald Reagan and Soviet leader Mikhail Gorbachev. It was at a crucial moment in the Cold War, with the United States and Soviet Union still at odds over issues ranging from arms control to economic philosophy. Van Cliburn concluded the program with "Russian Nights," a cherished song of the Russian nation, which he sang in Russian. Gorbachev was flooded with emotion hearing the beloved melody, burst into song, and embraced the American pianist with a generous embrace. *Music*, more effectively than any military weaponry, broke through the barriers of politics and conflict that had

Management as Music

previously fortified the diplomatic space between the two countries, dismantling years of built-up hate note by note.

A tour of our own life experiences only reinforces the cruciality of music within the tapestry of the human experience. New parents use lullabies as an initial way to bond with their newborns. Fast forward to the bookend of life, and we often find ourselves singing to those concluding their journey as a way of providing comfort and peace. And, in the space in between, music is a steadfast companion as we navigate heartbreaks and triumphs, loves lost and achievements attained, moments of profound connection and valleys where we "crawl into the space between the notes and curl (our) back to loneliness" (Maya Angelou).

> *"A tour of our own life experiences only reinforces the cruciality of music within the tapestry of the human experience"*

As my high school choir director and good friend Randy Edwards has often said, music is indeed the soundtrack of our lives.

Beyond providing a soundtrack, research reveals the medical and sociological benefits of music. From many examples to choose, here is a sampling:

An Overture: Bending Toward Beauty

- Just 16 minutes of listening to music can release sadness.[i]
- Students who take music lessons do better in science.[ii]
- Listening to music lowers blood pressure.[iii]
- The field of music therapy is a powerful tool to assist patients in healing from mental and physical injuries.

Most profoundly, researchers from the University of Utah discovered that the portion of the brain that interprets music is one of the last areas not totally decimated by the insidious disease of dementia.[iv] Music, therefore, is perhaps the final gleam of light to penetrate a labyrinth of darkness.

Ancient Greeks had the most expansive view of the power of music, believing that it could shape character (Aristotle) and that everything in the universe had a musical structure (Plato).[v] Plato summarized this mystical reach of music when he commented that music "gives a soul to the universe, wings to the mind, flight to the imagination, and life to everything." He also concluded that the "patterns in music ... are the keys to learning."

Researchers from Finland provided scientific backing to Plato's claims when they found that music activates the emotional, motor, and creative areas of the brain.[vi] It is not a stretch, then, to declare that music is one of the few forces-- if not the only force--that

"music activates the emotional, motor, and creative areas of the brain"

utilizes every portion of the human brain ... and heart. Perhaps composer Helen Kemp summarized it best: "Body, mind, spirit, voice. It takes the whole person to sing and rejoice!"

In his first Norton lecture at Harvard, composer, conductor, and educator Leonard Bernstein advocated for an interdisciplinary approach to learning (Artful Learning, as he phrased it). He proposed that all learning could be infused with the arts and that "the best way to know a thing is in the context of another discipline."[vii]

The pages that follow seek to follow Bernstein's model by claiming music as the most comprehensive managerial metaphor available to leaders.

*****

As we begin this journey, an introductory word about the structure and purpose of music will provide context to what follows.

Regarding structure:

- The production of music requires vibrations that flow through a vessel that are controlled with the purpose of creating emotion.

An Overture: Bending Toward Beauty

- Every note played/sung has a defined value (i.e., how long each note is held). Without giving notes value, music is chaotic and unplayable.
- In Western music, songs have a time signature and a key signature, denoting how many beats are in each measure and what key (or scale) the song is based upon.
- Music is relational. Each note's true beauty and potential is only revealed when combined with other notes. Notes in vertical relationship to each other make harmony possible, while notes in horizontal relationship allow for the creation of melody.
- The sound of every note must be continually renewed in terms of tuning pitch and creating vibrations.
- Music brings a unity of sound through diversity--a diversity of pitches, rhythms, and dynamics (i.e., how loud or soft musical notes are played). A shorthand definition of music could be the act of composing unity through diversity.

Applying this structure to management:

- Effective leadership results from *action* (vibration) that flows through *people* (vessels) with *strategy* (control) and defined *objectives* (emotion). Action, people, strategy, and objectives must all work in concert for our leadership to hit the mark.
- Each team member (note) must have value that is clearly defined. Leadership most often falters when team members do not perceive their value. Stephen

Covey said it best: "Leadership is communicating the worth and potential of people so clearly that they are inspired to see it in themselves." In fact, one test for leadership might be: Do our teams perceive that we are thinking of their needs when we are not *required* to think of their needs?

- Effective leaders provide a clear, unifying tone (vision). They also provide rhythm to their leadership that is dependable and easily understood by team members.
- Effective leadership is relational. Organizational melody and harmony are only composed by forming, cultivating, and nurturing healthy relationships with our team members.
- Effective leadership is always self-renewing. That is, there is a consistent renewing of strategy, objectives, relationships, skills, and vision.
- Effective leaders creatively leverage the diversity of their teams to form unity toward organizational objectives. Leaders must be reconcilers.

The anatomy of a note, therefore, shares common DNA with the anatomy of leadership. Both, when dissected, survive through the promotion of strategic action, value, relationships, renewal, and diversity. The following chapters offer practical advice in promoting these qualities within your team.

Finally, a note regarding the purpose of music. Jeremy Montagu, a professor from the University of Oxford who

An Overture: Bending Toward Beauty

specialized in the history of musical instruments, described the results of his years of study this way: "(I)t may be that the whole purpose of (early) music was cohesion, cohesion between parent and child, cohesion between father and mother, cohesion between one family and the next, and thus the creation of the whole organization of society."[viii]

More recently, acclaimed conductor Dr. Anton Armstrong concluded that "(m)aking music together is not just about the music." Rather, he observed that we make music to "feel connected to one another and to build community … (O)ur choral art may be one of the last social platforms where people can still come together, put aside those differences that so much of society uses to create barriers to divide people … (and) seek to build bridges to bring people together into community."[ix]

If the fundamental purpose of music through the ages has been cohesion, let us harvest those lessons to foster bonds that make our teams more unified, productive, efficient, and caring.

In so doing, we will not only grow stronger teams but also a stronger society. In our divided world, is there any greater calling?

CHAPTER 1

The Melodic Imperative and the Power of Story

The power of musical melody is undeniable. *Merriam-Webster* defines melody as "a sweet or agreeable succession or arrangement of sounds."

We are all familiar with "ear worm" melodies that burrow deep into our subconscious. Advertising executives have long recognized the power of musical jingles to sell products, and composers from Tin Pan Alley to the modern day have made lucrative careers in crafting melodies that linger in the heart long after they leave our ears.

But beyond the ear worm melodies that come and go, some melodies become so ingrained in us that, in an instant, we are transported back in time. It is these melodies that become the threads that weave our life stories together into a cohesive tapestry. D. H. Lawrence portrayed this idea elegantly in his poem "Piano":

Softly, in the dusk, a woman is singing to me;
Taking me back down the vista of years, till I see
A child sitting under the piano, in the boom of the tingling strings
And pressing the small, poised feet of a mother who smiles as she sings.

In spite of myself, the insidious mastery of song
Betrays me back, till the heart of me weeps to belong

1. The Melodic Imperative and the Power of Story

To the old Sunday evenings at home, with winter outside
And hymns in the cosy parlour, the tinkling piano our guide.

So now it is vain for the singer to burst into clamour
With the great black piano appassionato. The glamour
Of childish days is upon me, my manhood is cast
Down in the flood of remembrance, I weep like a child for the past.[x]

Just as a composer's primary agenda is to compose a melody that will imbed itself in the human heart, it is imperative for the effective manager to create indelible melodies for their teams.

Perhaps the most effective technique for managerial melody making is the use of storytelling. Storytelling is the Trojan Horse of leadership because it allows managers the opportunity to imbue values, emphases, and strategies without being pedantic or overbearing. It works by stealth, quietly cultivating a workplace ethos that provides

"our teams can learn what values we cherish by the stories we tell"

the nourishing soil for managerial objectives to grow and flourish. Just as children learn valuable life lessons by listening to unassuming fables, our teams can learn what values we cherish by the stories we tell.

Author Reynolds Price wrote eloquently of the deep human need for stories: "A need to tell and hear stories is essential to the species Homo sapiens--second in necessity apparently after nourishment and before love and shelter. Millions survive without love or home, almost none in silence …"[xi]

Recent research discovered that people's heart rates rose and fell in unison when listening to the same story. Professor Lucas Parra, senior author of the study put it this way: "It's the story that drives the heart. There's an explicit link between people's heart rates and a narrative."[xii]

Managerial stories can be *macro-narratives* (aimed at influencing your team as a whole) or *micro-narratives* (aimed at influencing individual team members). Macro-narratives are focused on promoting the overall managerial purposes, goals, objectives, and strategies and are told through mass communication (e.g., staff meetings, emails to the entire staff). Micro-narratives focus on connecting team members' individual stories to the larger managerial purposes, goals, objectives, and strategies and are told through one-to-one communications (personal emails, handwritten notes, individual conversations). The horizon where both macro and micro narratives meet is the heart of great leadership.

To have maximum impact, the stories managers tell, whether macro or micro, must: 1) feel natural and not contrived; 2) have an emotional connection to the listener; 3) have the intentional goal of moving the organization forward; and 4) be strategically aligned with the purposes, goals, objectives, and strategies of the organization.

1. The Melodic Imperative and the Power of Story

Natural, not contrived. If the world had to select one melody to represent the very best of human musical achievement, the vote would likely come down in favor of Beethoven's "Ode to Joy" from his Symphony No. 9. The irony is that the melody is extremely simple; in fact, "Ode to Joy" is one of the first melodies young pianists learn to play, as the rhythm and note pattern are easily learned.

Why, then, is Beethoven's melody rightly adored? Leonard Bernstein explained the brilliance of Beethoven's melody writing as "the inexplicable ability to know exactly what the next note has to be."

Beethoven was never considered a great melodist. His melodies produced no revolutionary innovations or required exquisite technical ability to execute. Rather, his greatness came because his melodies were completely natural. The result: His melodies were accessible to the listener but without being ordinary.

In the same way, managerial stories must be natural and not feel contrived. We should avoid mimicking the style of others and develop our own unique storytelling approach. At the center of natural storytelling is identifying what stories move us and then finding creative ways to communicate those stories to others.

Management as Music

Tip: Create a computer document or physical file where you collect stories you think will be useful in motivating your team. Notate on each story what specific qualities the story will reinforce in your team and what venue might be best to tell the story.

Emotional connection to the listener. John Steinbeck, in *East of Eden*, wrote: "If the story is not about the hearer, he will not listen … A great and interesting story is about everyone or will not last." If our colleagues do not see themselves in the stories we tell, those stories will have little lasting impact. When deciding what stories will resonate with our teams, it is imperative that we are active listeners. Take comprehensive notes of team members' ideas and interests, as these observations can later be the catalyst of meaningful connection with your teams. Perhaps have an index card file while you keep a card for every team member, noting their specific interests and life stories. Be eclectic in your story telling, drawing from personal experiences, history, current events, literature, popular culture, and organizational history.

Moving the narrative forward. Stephen Sondheim observed that "The Bench Scene" in the musical *Carousel* was the "singular most important moment in the evolution of contemporary musicals." In the age before *Carousel*, the songs in musicals did little (if anything) to advance the overall story being told. In fact, sometimes the songs had *nothing* to do with the story at all! Instead, the songs were a

1. The Melodic Imperative and the Power of Story

break in the story--a moment for everyone to catch their breath. "The Bench Scene" was radical in that it intentionally and effectively used song to propel the story forward. The song was imperative in the telling of the story, not merely a space filler. Composers of musical theater ever since have made songs an integral piece in the arch of the story being told.

For managers, every story told must be calibrated to move forward organizational purposes, goals, objectives, and strategies. Of every story told, managers should ask: How is this story moving the organization forward? Every story must have a vision of what is to be accomplished.

"every story told must be calibrated to move forward organizational purposes"

Strategic alignment. The melodies managers create should not be flowery decoration; rather, they must be carefully crafted to serve and support the larger organizational purposes, goals, objectives, and strategies.

More specifically, purposes answer why the organization exists; goals answer where it is going; objectives answer what must be accomplished to get there; and strategies answer how to achieve such results. Each story should support either the purposes, goals, objectives, or strategies of the organizations; otherwise, the story is not worth telling.

Management as Music

Tips: Create a spreadsheet of the stories you have told your team, and label whether the story served the purposes, goals, objectives, or strategies of the organization. Notate the reaction you received to the story (both positive and negative). Also, have as a regular portion of management meetings a discussion of whether the management team is effectively driving the narrative of the organization.

*****

The bottom line: Music influences more effectively than any lecture could because music aims straight for the heart by telling stores.

Storytelling is embedded into the human brain and, therefore, it is inevitable that each organization will have stories being told about it daily. The task for mangers is to ensure that those stories (melodies) have messages that promote the organization's purposes, goals, objectives, and strategies. Or, put another way, managers should frequently ask themselves: Am I shaping the melody for my team, or is my team's melody shaping me?

Leaders who fail to drive the narrative within their teams relinquish the single most effective tool they have as leaders.

CHAPTER 2

The Humility of Harmony

Merriam-Webster defines harmony as "the combination of simultaneous notes in a chord ... (a) pleasing arrangement of parts ... an interweaving of different accounts into a single narrative."

The basic components of harmony, therefore, can be summarized as a unity of different *pitches*, a unity of *rhythm*, and a unity of *purpose*. Only when all three components work in combination is harmony achieved.

From a music theory standpoint, the individual notes within a harmony make no sense without the other component notes. Imagine, for example, the bewilderment of an audience if one member of a barbershop quartet started singing their line without the other three. It takes each note--in delicate balance and in shared rhythm and purpose--to create a rich and rewarding effect. In essence, each note performs an act of bravery by sublimating itself to the overall harmonic goal (the "single narrative," as *Webster* calls it). At bottom, creating harmony is the art of reconciliation, and at the heart of that reconciliation is humility. *Humility forms the foundation for harmony.*

Implications for the manager. We live in inharmonious times, where almost every portion of American life is factionalized, disconnected, and tribalized. Some prominent examples:

(1) Political parties are becoming more ideologically pure, with little emphasis on compromise.

(2) Churches have ceased to be places where diverse views gather to worship together. Rather, research shows churches have become homogenized, where people of similar viewpoints congregate.

(3) Wireless communication has made face-to-face communication less relevant in business, medicine, education, and even personal relationships. We can go to school, work, have a doctor's visit, and even end a relationship with the click of a mouse!

Lurking beneath all of this is a public dialogue that can only be characterized as coarse and divisive. Fueled by the anonymity of the internet and the proliferation of social media, our debates on every imaginable topic devolve quickly into shouting matches--two sides yelling fruitlessly over a chasm.

The source of these divisions can be linked to our increasing isolation and disconnectedness from one another. In *Bowling Alone,* sociologist Robert Putnam clearly defined the problem, describing it as America's "declining social capital."

2. The Humility of Harmony

For the manager, creating harmony in our work teams is much like creating musical harmony. It does not require everyone to agree (play in unison). It only requires that we play together (in community with each other), in a shared rhythm, and with a common purpose.

When there is true harmony within a team, the individual members brush away thoughts of who gets credit for success; no one is auditioning for a solo or rushing to have their moment under the spotlight. Rather, everyone steps out in humility, confident that their colleagues will provide nurturing support. *Humility is the key to harmony.*

> *"When there is true harmony within a team, the individual members brush away thoughts of who gets credit"*

Consider the following strategies for cultivating harmony in the workplace:

Be intentional in the way you organize and decorate your office. Many leaders crowd their walls with certificates of achievement, creating museums of past accomplishments. But these professional adornments pull our faces to the past instead of point us to the future; they also can foster silent resentment, constructing an invisible wall between the manager and their teams.

Management as Music

A more effective approach is to transform your individual workspace into a showcase to servanthood, displaying quotes that move you, pictures of mentors who have inspired you, or paintings/pictures that reflect your overall theory of leadership. These showcases of servanthood can be conversation starters with your team that allow you to express your managerial priorities and organizational objectives.

An example of office art used to promote managerial values might look something like this sample message:

My favorite painting is The Sower at Sunset by Vincent van Gogh. It's a pastoral scene of a farmer sowing his crop, and a print of it hangs in my office. I've always liked the painting because it seemed to represent in a simple way our roles on this earth—to sow hope, encouragement, friendship. But during this time of quarantine I've had the opportunity to stare on the painting more and more, and further lessons have emerged.

First, you'll notice the sun is behind the sower, and he is walking away from it. But despite the setting sun, he walks confidently forward to finish the task in front of him. In fact, he almost has a boldness to his stride. The takeaway for me? Often in our journey we have just a glimmer of light and that light might seem like a distant gleam. But if we have confidence in our mission, we can forge ahead with inspiration to finish the task before us.

Second, the sower is alone, and he is almost engulfed in the vastness of his fields. There is no help in sight, no crew to back him up, no equipment to lighten the load. Here the lesson is that life frequently finds us making our journeys physically alone and with more work to do than seems possible—this is especially true in our days of quarantine! However, despite our physical separation from others, we must never lose sight that we can still do valuable work that will reap benefits down the line. Our individual contributions really do matter!

Third, we don't see where the sower is headed—the rest of his journey (his future) is a mystery. This is a perfect metaphor, because none of us know what the future holds, but life demands that we continue to be sowers even though we are not certain of the ending. In fact, we may never see the results of the seeds we sow.

Lastly, you can see the sower's mature crop behind him. The lesson here is that our work of sowing is never complete. Even when our crops are ready to harvest, there is still sowing to be done.

Learn the stories — the narratives — of your team members. There is a concept in the medical field called "narrative medicine." The basic idea is that every patient has a story that goes beyond the symptoms they bring to the doctor's office. These stories can shed light on how the patient became ill, the tipping point that compelled them to seek help, and the challenges they might face in getting better. Just so, when managers seek to learn the narratives of their team members, they bond with their team members and equip themselves with valuable information that will allow them to be more effective leaders.

Management as Music

Tip: Keep a computer file or physical file where you record important information about the life stories of your team members (e.g., the names of their children, where they grew up, their hobbies).

Promote and practice humble communication. Humble communication requires that we place ourselves in the background. E. B. White and William Strunk, Jr., in their classic *The Elements of Style*, presented this idea well when they suggested that we "(w)rite in a way that draws the reader's attention to the sense and substance of the writing, rather than to the mood and temper of the author."

In terms of practical application, humble communication requires scrubbing any hint of defensiveness, condescension, or hyperbole from our communication, as these only put ourselves in the fore, distract listeners from our goals, and create unneeded resentment.

More specifically, defensiveness suggests a lack of confidence in our decision making, which raises concerns about our competence in meeting the needs of our teams. Condescension devalues the importance of our team members, creating cracks in team solidarity. Hyperbolic, exaggerated language--either in the negative ("this is the worst ...") or the positive ("this is the best ...") gives a false sense of reality, and healthy growth only occurs when we have a realistic view of the environment we inhabit.

2. The Humility of Harmony

Further, be aware of non-verbal communication that distracts from your message. For example, avoid at all cost crossing your arms or tapping your fingers/feet repeatedly during meetings, as these gestures signal disinterest (at best) or contempt (at worst). Be intentional about making eye contact with everyone speaking at meetings; this simple act is an outward reflection that you value the contributions of your colleagues. Nodding your head at appropriate times and showing open palms while speaking can also be powerful non-verbal cues showing that you value the speaker/listener.

One powerful non-verbal action leaders can use to promote humility is to give up perks associated with their managerial position. Examples include relinquishing a prime parking spot or office space. These types of actions go a long way in communicating humility to our teams.

Additional strategies: Give every member of your team Strunk and White's *The Elements of Style* and Dale Carnegie's *How to Win Friends and Influence People* as primers on humble communication techniques. Send out regular emails specifically on the topic of communication, outlining strategies for becoming more effective communicators. Solicit feedback from team members about their communication best practices, and share the results with your whole team. Recommend podcasts, articles, webinars on communication to your teams.

Management as Music

Effective communication is humble communication. The two are inextricably bound.

Model and encourage brave leadership. In the work setting, brave leadership occurs when someone risks professional reputation, organizational influence, popularity, or even job security to defend a colleague or promote an idea. Research shows that leaders who exhibit bravery and courage at work influence their coworkers to act with bravery as well.[xiii]

Bravery and humility are really synonyms, for when leaders step forth in bravery, they elevate the needs of others above themselves. They also promote solidarity within their teams--and solidarity is the bedrock of effective team building.

*****

Humble leadership can be reduced to this: Do we conform our jobs to fit our own preferences, or do we conform our preferences to fit our jobs? Do we use our positions to promote ourselves, or do we use our positions to promote the objectives of the organizations and teams we serve? A humble leader is forever removing barriers between themselves and their

"A humble leader is forever removing barriers between themselves and their teams..."

2. The Humility of Harmony

teams, always using the organization's goals--and the needs of their teams--as the guiding light.

An avatar for this type of humble leadership is Dean Smith, who coached the University of North Carolina Tar Heels basketball team for 36 seasons, where he modeled daily the transformative power of humility to create harmony within a team. Humility pervaded every aspect of Smith's philosophy of coaching and life. Of many examples to choose, a small sampling:

To emphasize teamwork over individual achievement, Smith implemented a policy that every player who scored would point to the player who provided the assist ("thanking the passer"). When flying commercial, he made all of the coaches sit in the back and let the tallest players sit in first class so they would not be cramped during the flight. He kept up with all of his players, acknowledging their birthdays, attending each of their weddings, remembering the names of their children, and sending them yearly reports on the current team with attached handwritten notes. He interrupted whatever he was doing if a player entered his office. He never cursed or used belittling language, fearing it would distract from his message. In his will he requested that each of his former players be sent a $200 check to "enjoy a dinner out compliments of Coach Smith."

Management as Music

My favorite Coach Smith story: When player Makhtar N'Diaye, whose hometown was in Africa, was struggling in practice, Smith sat him down and asked if something was bothering him. Was he homesick, injured, tired? N'Diaye answered without making eye contact. Smith countered: "Mak, look at me when I'm talking to you." N'Diaye responded: "Coach, in my culture to look an adult in the eye is a sign of disrespect." Instead of rebuking N'Diaye, Smith did something remarkable: he sent assistant coach Bill Guthridge to N'Diaye's hometown in Africa to learn more about the customs of his culture so that the coaching staff could become more effective teachers.

And Smith did it all without drawing attention to himself. When asked why he did not take credit for his role in integrating North Carolina restaurants in the 1960's, he responded: "You should never be proud of doing the right thing. You should just do it."

To a person, Smith's former players adored him--not because of his winning record but because of his *humility*. His actions were always calibrated to serve his team, not himself. The headline of the *Chicago Sun-Times* announcing his death said it all: "Dean Smith: Humble, Dignified, Remembered Well by All."

*****

2. The Humility of Harmony

There is a reconciling imperative at the heart of effective leadership. The world yearns for leaders who will use their influence to unite the diverse threads of humanity toward common goals. Music teaches that this reconciling work--this work of creating harmony--requires ultimate humility.

Humble, reconciling leaders--like great harmonists--see beyond the individual building blocks of life and instead look toward what those building blocks can become when joined together for a united purpose.

Humility is at the core of musical harmony. It is also at the core of every great leader. To lead with humility without relinquishing authority is the challenge of every thoughtful leader.

CHAPTER 3

In Praise of Wurlitzers

When the accomplished Chinese pianist Liu Shih-Kun was asked about his practice regimen, he responded that his piano of choice was a battered German upright, explaining that "on a poor piano you try harder and so perform better."

I share Shih-Kun's appreciation for old uprights. As a child I learned to play on a vintage black Wurlitzer--the same piano my mother practiced on as a child. My mom did not come from a musical family; her parents did not read music or carry a tune. But they wisely saw music as a way of expanding the geography of her imagination, transporting her beyond the confines of the small town where they lived. Enter the black Wurlitzer. It was a mess of a piano. It never held a pitch, the notes sometimes stuck, and each key required a different level of pressure to fully activate. It was a world away from the Steinway grand that I sometimes practiced on in the sanctuary of my church.

There were times I wished our old Wurlitzer would morph into that Steinway--every note effortless, every pitch perfect, every tone blended. Alas, no magical transformation ever occurred. Instead, our Wurlitzer only became more faded, growing old watching me grow, just at it had watched over my mother years before. But it did more than that. The

3. In Praise of Wurlitzers

scratched and faded Wurlitzer taught me the imperative of sensitive musicianship through embracing imperfection.

At the same moment I was learning the physical landscape of the keyboard, the imperfections of the Wurlitzer demanded that I also develop an individualized approach to every key. It was as if the keys possessed souls, imbued with unique personalities, preferences, and sensibilities. And my job was to respect the differences of each note while simultaneously uniting them with the differences of the others. Talk about a musical balancing act! I will never be considered a great pianist--but I am a *sensitive* pianist, and I owe that to my mother's Wurlitzer.

In 2017, there were 1,000 damaged musical instruments that resided in "instrument graveyards" within the Philadelphia Public School System--cracked cellos, horns with broken valves, flutes that leaked. The schools simply had no funds to fix them. A group of civic leaders commissioned a Pulitzer Prize-winning composer, David Lang, to create a symphony using the broken instruments. Each instrument was recorded, and the composer used those individual sounds—those *broken* sounds—to complete the composition. They called it the "Symphony for a Broken Orchestra."[xiv]

The "Symphony for a Broken Orchestra" is really a metaphor of what management can be at its best. Like the piano keys on my mother's Wurlitzer, all of us are broken

Management as Music

in our own unique ways. We each have imperfections that sometimes make our songs seem out of tune, especially when we're all alone on the stage with the spotlight shining brightly on us. Our imperfections can even result in a sense of paralysis that prevents us from taking risks.

But managers, acting with the heart of a musician, can motivate our teams to shelve fears of being imperfect and join other imperfect instruments in a unified purpose. The result: A perfect sound that honors the best in humanity. It is the lesson of the "Symphony for a Broken Orchestra." It is the lesson of my mother's Wurlitzer.

CHAPTER 4

The Secret of Relative Pitch

There is a common misconception about the musical concept of perfect pitch (also known as absolute pitch). Many assume the term refers to singing "in tune." The proper meaning of perfect pitch, however, is the ability to produce a given musical note without the benefit of a reference tone. Put more simply, it is the ability to produce a particular note out of thin air--on the spot!--without any reference notes to help you get there.

In contrast, relative pitch is the ability to produce (or identify) a pitch when given a reference pitch. Perfect pitch is rare, while relative pitch can often be developed through dedicated musical study.

One might assume that perfect pitch is a key to superb musicianship. But directors will tell you that the success of a choir relies less on having a single singer with perfect pitch than having a core group with strong relative pitch. And the same is true for leading others.

Managers naturally strive to produce decisions and outcomes that hit the mark every time (i.e., perfect pitch). This is an unhealthy expectation that inevitably leads to disappointment and even disillusionment. A healthier

Management as Music

approach is to strive for relative pitch, where past experience informs and instructs future decision making.

But how do we cultivate relative pitch? The answer lies in promoting a workplace culture that values self-reflection. Specifically, team members must have a realistic view of:

> *"The answer lies in promoting a workplace culture that values self-reflection"*

- their individual job duties;
- their own strengths and weaknesses;
- how their position fits into the larger organization;
- the organization's overall purpose and goals; and
- the larger environment the organization inhabits.

Self-reflection is not a natural human enterprise. G. K. Chesterton, in *The Man Who Was Thursday*, expressed well how humans only see a portion of the whole: "Shall I tell you the secret of the world? It is that we only know the back of the world. We see everything from behind … That is not a tree, but the back of a tree. That is not a cloud, but the back of a cloud. Cannot you see that everything is stopping and hiding a face? If we could only get round in front--"[xv]

When astronauts look back at Earth from space, they experience what is called an "Overview Effect." It represents a heightened appreciation of the fragility of life and how humans are interconnected with each other.

4. The Secret of Relative Pitch

But few become astronauts. For most, we simply muddle along, seeing only part of the bigger picture, only reading our individual part of the larger musical score. The managerial puzzle, of course, is how to create an "Overview Effect" for ourselves and our teams. That is: How do we promote a culture that values reading the *whole score* and not merely our individual parts?

At the most basic level, self-reflection can be classified into four categories: internal, external, vertical, and horizontal. Internal self-reflection is initiated by the individual, while external self-reflection is initiated by others. Vertical self-reflection indicates how accurately an employee views their role within the context of the entire organization, while horizontal self-reflection reflects how accurately the employee understands the specific requirements of their job. The ideal is that all four types of reflection work in combination.

One approach to promoting internal self-reflection is keeping a daily journal that outlines work successes and failures. Researchers Francesca Gino and Bradley Staats, for example, found that workers improved their performance by as much as 20% when they spent time at the end of the day reflecting (e.g., discussing what went wrong, what went right). [xvi] Frequently share journal entries with your team, and encourage them to keep journals as well. I suggest daily journal entries have at least

33

one statement that analyzes the past (retrospective), one statement that assesses the present, and one statement that looks toward the future (prospective).

A method for promoting external self-reflection is using intentional and frequent communication that reinforces how team members' work fits into the overall mission of the organization. I suggest keeping a spreadsheet of all team members and documenting the times (and methods) you communicated with them how their specific contributions have influenced organizational goals. This will provide a visual guide in gauging whether you have employed external self-reflection on a frequent and distributed basis.

Additional strategies:

- Incorporate reflection at meetings. Have standing questions for your teams, which might include: What was my biggest work challenge this week? What was my greatest work success this week?
- Frequently share news/trends that affect your organization that goes *beyond* your team members' job descriptions. This may include articles about the larger environment in which your organization operates.
- Subscribe to newsletters/trade journals/blogs that relate to your organization, and encourage your teams to do the same.

4. The Secret of Relative Pitch

- Write a managerial obituary, outlining the qualities you want to be remembered for as a leader. Have your team do the same. Regularly revisit this document, editing and updating as necessary. This exercise will help crystallize managerial goals and assist in evaluating whether those goals are being actualized. The piece entitled "My Three Pillars of Leadership" in the Appendix is an example of such a managerial obituary.
- Have your teams participate in personality testing (such as the Enneagram test, the Myers Briggs Type Indicator, the DISC Personality Test, the Eysenck personality test, the Hogan Personality Inventory, and the Keirsey Temperament Sorter). These tests will help your teams think more deeply about their strengths, motivations, and preferences.
- Be intentional in having all members of your team lead training, not just those who have a natural aptitude for teaching. Ideally, team members will perform some type of teaching annually. Teaching is perhaps the best developer of self-reflection, as it quickly uncovers weaknesses and strengths.
- On an annual basis have your team members complete an analysis where they identify the strengths, weaknesses, opportunities, and threats of the organization--and themselves.
- Find at least one work mentor who can be an honest sounding board when you have questions. Encourage your team to find mentors as well.

- Create short-term opportunities for team members to perform the job duties of other team members. This will allow your team to learn new skills and gain a broader understanding of the organization.
- Tell stories about your organization's history and figures who have influenced the organization. Perhaps create a regular email entitled "Servant Sketches," where you describe the influence of organizational heroes.

Educational pioneer John Dewey observed that "(w)e do not learn from experience ... we learn from reflecting on experience." A lack of self-reflection is at the heart of most poor performance and poor decision making. Our teams are only as strong as their ability to see themselves and their environments realistically. Self-reflection is the single most important quality we can promote in our teams--and ourselves--and it provides the largest return on investment of any managerial tool.

CHAPTER 5

Embracing the Beauty of Dissonance

Leonard Bernstein's *West Side Story* is built around the "Devil's Interval" (the musical interval called a tritone). It is the most dissonant of intervals (harsh to the ear), and composers generally avoid it.[xvii] But Bernstein challenged listeners to find meaning and beauty within the dissonance. The result was one of the most celebrated musicals of all time.

A human example of embracing dissonance is Andrew Solomon's *Far from the Tree,* a nonfiction masterpiece that tells the stories of parents raising children far different from themselves.[xviii] After interviewing more than 300 families of exceptional children, Solomon found that these parents discovered unexpected meaning and fulfillment from the uniqueness of their children. Solomon's conclusion was simple, yet profound: Diversity in humanity is the uniting thread that binds us all.

Growing up I felt "far from the tree." My father was an accomplished high school athlete and liked by all. He aced the ACT and was president of everything. In contrast, I was usually the last to be picked for sporting competitions and was the quintessential introvert. I only ran for one position in my school career and lost in dramatic fashion! Most

Management as Music

afternoons you could find me quietly practicing Chopin etudes on the piano, far away from any glaring crowd.

But instead of making me feel self-conscious in the ways that he and I were different, my father embraced those differences. One moment tells the story: On the night before he succumbed to cancer, we had a final conversation in his hospital room. His final words to me were to continue playing the piano. One of the regrets of his life, he said, was not learning how to play. He said I had a gift and that I should nurture that gift. To an awkward teenager, this affirmation of my uniqueness instilled confidence and was a blessing to forge a life path that diverged from his own.

How can we lead our teams to appreciate the gift of dissonance?

- By encouraging our teams to be futurists when others are stuck in the present or past. I suggest managers infuse every meeting with at least one element that discusses the future. A helpful question here might be: "What threats will our organization face in the next year? Five years?"
- By being intentional in hiring team members with diverse backgrounds. Research has consistently shown that diverse teams make better decisions.
- By applauding and highlighting team members who have the courage to push back on conventional

5. Embracing the Beauty of Dissonance

thinking. Forage your organizational history to highlight those who have been dissonant voices.
- By consistently challenging our teams with opinions that cut against the consensus of the group. I suggest managers perform a self-check weekly, asking: "How have I challenged my team this week?" Encourage your managerial colleagues to hold you accountable when not challenging your team.
- By exposing our vulnerabilities to our teams, modeling how dissonance can blend toward beauty. At every manager meeting ask: "What mistakes have we made this week? How can we learn from those mistakes?"
- By giving those with undervalued skill sets a platform to teach and train other team members.
- By creating a diversity, equity, and inclusion statement for your organization that clearly delineates how your organization benefits from diversity. Regularly share and discuss this statement with your team.

To summarize: Managers must make the acceptance, promotion, and cultivation of dissonance a hallmark of their leadership style. Meetings, written communications, and evaluations must all be aligned in supporting a workplace ethos that values the need for dissonance as a balancing corrective to organizational conformity and "group think."

Leaders must cultivate dissonance to balance conformity

Management as Music

More than a quarter century after my father's death, I still play Chopin etudes. But now, thanks to my father, I appreciate even more how the dissonant chords resolve into surprised beauty.

The summons for leaders: Will we challenge our teams--and ourselves--to find beauty in dissonance?

CHAPTER 6

Managing Modulations

The term modulation in music theory is defined as a transitioning from one musical key to another key.

Whether it is transitioning into new job duties or shepherding teams through changes in strategy or priorities, managers navigate various *workplace modulations* on a daily basis. Music theory provides the manager sage guidance on how to handle these delicate transitions.

Lesson one. Perhaps the most common technique for crafting a musical modulation is the use of a pivot chord (a chord that belongs to both the home key and the new key). Pivot chords provide smooth modulations because the new key utilizes a familiar foundation (i.e., chord) from the old key.

The lesson here is that managers must find opportunities to connect changes/transitions with a past that is familiar. This can be accomplished in several ways:

- By emphasizing that the values, processes, or strategies are staying the same.
- By emphasizing how new changes are similar to past values, processes, or strategies.

Management as Music

- By emphasizing how new changes are in harmony with past values, processes, or strategies.
- By emphasizing how team members' past contributions are vital in pivoting from old to new processes.

Lesson two. Musical modulations are often incremental, transitioning from a home key to a key that is closely related to the home key. The takeaway for managers is that transitions are often handled best when implemented incrementally.

One of the greatest role models of leadership in the world of sports—or any world! —was UCLA basketball coach John Wooden. Not only were his teams champions year after year, he also won while teaching his players the value of teamwork, discipline, and preparation.

At the beginning of each season, Wooden began his inaugural practice with a lesson on the importance of shoes and socks. Seems silly, right? He explained his philosophy this way:

"I think it's the little things that really count. The first thing I would show our players at our first meeting was how to take a little extra time putting on their shoes and socks properly. The most important part of your equipment is your shoes and socks. You play on a hard floor. So you must have shoes that fit right. And you must not permit your socks to have wrinkles around the little toe—where you

6. Managing Modulations

generally get blisters—or around the heels. It took just a few minutes, but I did show my players how I wanted them to do it ... (T)hat's just a little detail that coaches must take advantage of, because it's the little details that made the big things come about."

The advice to "think big" is ubiquitous, but managers should never forget that the little things--especially during times of transition--really do count. Small acts of preparation are the backbone for our future success. Small acts of kindness form the bedrock of fruitful relationships. Small acts of affirmation foster confidence in others. But it also goes the other way. Small words of belittlement can ruin friendships. Small acts of giving up can lead to hopelessness.

"Small acts of preparation are the backbone for our future success"

A study from the Harvard Business School found that "(o)f all the things that can boost emotions, motivation and perceptions during a workday, the single most important is making progress in meaningful work. And the more frequently people experience that sense of progress, the more likely they are to be creatively productive in the long run."[xix]

The lesson? Managers should find small ways to show their team members that they are consistently making progress to individual or collective goals.

Management as Music

Put another way, the managerial task is to ask of ourselves and our teams: How are my small acts furthering the goals of the organization? How are my small acts furthering my own professional development?

Lesson three. While most composers begin by modulating to a higher key, there is also beauty when modulating to a lower key. The composer/arranger Dr. Mack Wilberg, for example, is brilliant in bringing texture, suspense, and beauty to a piece by modulating *downward*. The listener – and singer! – experiences a heightened exhilaration and meaning because Wilberg dared to defy their musical expectations.

A human example of the beauty of modulating downward is the life of author Henri Nouwen. Nouwen wrote an essay entitled "Finding Vocation in Downward Mobility" where he traced his initial attempts to please his parents by going to the "right" schools and teaching at the "right" universities.

Nouwen eventually reached the pinnacle of academic success, gaining tenure at a prestigious university. But this path left him unfulfilled. He ultimately found his true vocational calling not in the lecture halls of the Ivy League but by giving up the trappings of a tenured professorship to work in a community of profoundly disabled individuals. There he was charged with caring for a man named Adam, who needed full-time assistance to perform even the most basic functions.

6. Managing Modulations

In the act of serving Adam, Nouwen realized "that Adam, the weakest among us, created community. It was he who brought us together; his needs and his vulnerability made us into a true community ... His weakness became our strength. His weakness made us into a loving community. His weakness invited us to forgive one another, to calm our arguments ..." By serving the needs of others, Nouwen found true vocation.

Just so, managers can find their vocational calling by modulating downward and meeting the deeper needs of their colleagues. Writer Frederick Buechner put it best when he described vocation as "the place where our deep gladness meets the world's deep need."

When managers modulate downward and creatively defy the expectations of their teams by becoming servants, they gain credibility, attain new perspective, foster relationships necessary for future success, and ultimately find vocational fulfillment.

Lesson four. While most modulations aim for a smooth transition from old to new key, some happen abruptly, without preparation. These are called abrupt, direct, or phrase modulations. The advantage of an abrupt modulation is that it can quickly infuse energy and intensity into a composition, propelling the music forward in new and exciting directions.

Management as Music

Managers naturally prefer that changes are accompanied by extended periods of preparation. But there are times when abrupt, quick, decisive actions--actions without elaborate buildup, research, or buy-in--are needed to motivate our teams. These abrupt managerial modulations are most often effective when:

- The organization needs an infusion of energy, new thinking, or creativity; or
- The organization is presented with a crisis that needs decisive action.

A brilliant example of an abrupt modulation was how NASA responded to early tragedy. Apollo 1 was the original crew selected to land the first human on the moon. Tragically, on January 27, 1967, a cabin fire during a launch rehearsal killed all three crew members—Commander Gus Grissom, Ed White, and Roger Chaffee.

In the wake of this tragedy, it would have been quite natural for NASA to back off—or even abandon—its goal of landing a man on the moon before 1970. But instead of retreat, NASA used the crisis to reshape its whole philosophy. Specifically, NASA: 1) was straightforward about what led to the tragedy, 2) reworked its protocol, 3) developed a new mindset of toughness and competence, and 4) pushed forward with renewed determination.

6. Managing Modulations

Three days after the fire, Mission Control director Gene Kranz gave the following speech, which subsequently became the guiding force of NASA's philosophy: "From this day forward, Flight Control will be known by two words: Tough and Competent. Tough means we are forever accountable for what we do or what we fail to do. We will never again compromise our responsibilities … Competent means we will never take anything for granted … Mission Control will be perfect. When you leave this meeting today you will go to your office and the first thing you will do there is to write Tough and Competent on your blackboards. It will never be erased. Each day when you enter the room, these words will remind you of the price paid by Grissom, White, and Chaffee. These words are the price of admission to the ranks of Mission Control."

The result of NASA's reshaped commitment? On July 24, 1969, Apollo 11 landed safely on the moon.

Or consider the response to the sinking of the *Titanic*. The familiar background: A seemingly unsinkable luxury ship perished after hitting an iceberg, resulting in 1,500 lives lost. What you might not know is the backstory of how two ships, the *Californian* and the *Carpathia*, responded during the crisis.

The *Californian* was the closest ship to the *Titanic*, approximately 15 miles away. But the *Californian's* captain initially ignored the *Titanic's* distress rockets, viewing them as "company rockets" (signals between ships

Management as Music

from the same line). It was not until the next morning that the captain had the wireless officers inquire further, discovering the horrible truth that the *Titanic* was sinking. To complicate the situation, when the captain eventually changed the ship's course, he decided not to take a direct route but an alternate, cautious route. By the time the *Californian* reached the dying ship, it could be of little help.

The *Carpathia* was 58 miles away. Upon hearing the *Titanic's* first distress signal at 12:25 a.m., the crew immediately notified the captain. The captain ordered a reverse course to make all speed for the sinking ocean liner. All non-essential power was shut down, and engines were pushed beyond capacity. The state room was converted to a first aid room and other preparations were made to house the survivors. The captain also made a wise tactical decision—to chart a new course *before* he had calculated the two ships' relative positions. Later, once the ship was on the way, the captain calculated the *Titanic's* exact position and adjusted course. The result: The *Carpathia* was the first ship to assist the sinking *Titanic*, saving more than 700 lives.

Many lessons can be drawn, but I want to focus on three ways the *Carpathia* effectively responded to crisis, providing us a model for effective abrupt modulations.

First, the *Carpathia* did not wait for precise calculations before it started the rescue. Rather, it headed toward the wreckage immediately at full throttle, later adjusting the

6. Managing Modulations

course as needed. Crisis can lead to a paralysis of decision making. But often the best response to crisis is to head straight toward it with a dogged determination to meet the challenge head on.

Second, every member of the *Carpathia* played a role in the rescue. Each crew member pitched in, regardless of title, and everyone was considered a necessary component in responding to the disaster. Here we learn no one has the strength, skill, or energy to meet a crisis alone. It truly takes a team mindset to combat a crisis.

> *"It truly takes a team mindset to combat a crisis"*

Third, anyone can make a difference. The *Carpathia* was considered a third-rate ocean liner. It had no famous passengers, and its launch made no headlines. Instead, it was considered a "work horse" ship. But the lesson of the *Carpathia* is that anyone can make important contributions, especially during crisis circumstances.

The question for leaders: Are we leading our teams like the *Californian* or the *Carpathia*?

CHAPTER 7

Descants and the Intentionality of Inspiration

A descant is an independent melody sung or played above a basic melody. Etymologically, the word means a voice (*cantus*) above the other voices. A well-crafted descant can transform a pedestrian affair into a transcendent moment of inspiration.

The basic elements of a descant include:
- The descant melody works in deference to the main melody but it also works in harmony with the main melody.
- Descants typically occur in the final chorus or verse of a composition.
- Descants give a sense of emotional energy to a composition.

It is natural for managers to become absorbed with the mundane tasks of managing and forget that they have a *responsibility* to inspire--to create descant moments--for their teams. Inspiration is an indispensable component of leadership.

We often think of inspiration as being hit by a random bolt of lightning. In reality, inspiration results from planning, keeping an open mind, and pure hard work--it must be

7. Descants and the Intentionality of Inspiration

intentional. Here are suggestions on creating a culture of inspiration for your workplace:

First, practice continual self-reflection and identify what type of moments you finding inspiring. Maintain a file folder, computer file, or notebook where you record inspirational moments for later use. Keep an inspirational journal where you probe the themes that inspire your life. The main point here is that once your own inspirational trigger points are identified, you are in a posture to find creative ways to imbue that emotional energy to your team.

Second, make inspiration a habit. Find venues where you can inspire your teams on a regular basis. This can mean a recurring inspirational email, a standing segment in your monthly staff meeting, or regular handwritten notes to your staff. The form of this communication is less important than the fact that it is consistent and heartfelt.

Third, notice others in your workplace who are inspirational forces and encourage and empower them to keep it up. Whether this recognition is in a public setting or through private communication (like a handwritten note), managers should recognize those composing descants quietly behind the scenes. The keys here are that the recognition recognizes individual acts (as opposed generalized group accomplishments) and that you make this type of recognition on a regular basis. Further, be explicit in how

Management as Music

the contributions are furthering the overall mission and vision of the organization.

Lastly, remember that the most important descant you can craft is through the way you live your life. If your own life descant is not in harmony with the melody you are trying to create, you will fall short every time.

Composer Stephen Sondheim was once asked why singer Barbara Cook was such an adept interpreter of his songs. Sondheim replied: "She lives the lyric," meaning that she so thoroughly internalized the lyrics that she transformed herself into a living embodiment of the lyrics being sung. Sondheim added that "living the lyric" doe not come through spontaneity or even through pure talent but rather though a relentless dedication to the craft.

A case study in inspiration: One of my heroes is someone I have never met. Her name is Emma Hall, and she was a crossing guard at my son's elementary school in Louisiana. She became somewhat of a local celebrity because she waved and smiled to every single car and pedestrian that passed. She literally *never* stopped waving and smiling for several hours a day. Day after day, month after month, year after year she kept up a steady drumbeat of gratitude. The result: It was impossible not to feel uplifted after seeing her. Here was a person who composed a descant of inspiration wave by wave. Emma Hall "lived the lyric."

7. Descants and the Intentionality of Inspiration

The call for leaders: How will we "live the lyric" with our teams?

CHAPTER 8

The Pentatonic Scale and the Sanctity of Safe Spaces

As a young pianist, I loved composing songs using only the black keys on the piano. Regardless of the notes I played, the sounds blended! This type of experimentation in a safe environment provided me confidence as I ventured to play in key signatures that were less forgiving.

Music theory provides an explanation for this phenomenon: The five black notes on the piano form a pentatonic scale. The pentatonic scale has no semitones, which means that there is no tension between the notes in the scale. In a normal seven note major scale, the fourth and seventh notes introduce suspense and tension; when these notes are taken away, dissonance is eliminated.

Modern music educators, especially those using the Orff and Waldorf methodologies, rely heavily on the pentatonic scale to develop creativity and improvisation in children, as the nature of the scale prevents any real harmonic miscues. In this laboratory of improvisation, children gain confidence, hone skills, and learn their strengths and weaknesses as musicians.

But it is not only musicians who need safe places to develop--it also applies to the notes they create! Acoustic

8. The Pentatonic Scale and the Sanctity of Safe Spaces

instruments, for example, require a certain degree of space for the sounds they create to fully resonate.

Applications for leadership. Managers have a responsibility to provide this type of safe space of experimentation for our teams. More specifically, there are at least five types of safe spaces managers must construct to promote a healthy workplace ethos.

Safe space to offer opinions. A fatal blow to team morale occurs when members are either afraid to express opinions or think their opinions will be summarily dismissed without any meaningful consideration. Effective managers not only politely accept and consider team members' opinions, they actively seek out other viewpoints, especially those viewpoints that might offer contrasting perspective.

One approach for promoting opinion sharing is for managers to proactively solicit opinions from team members. By initiating the opinion sharing process, managers gain credibility with their teams.

Tip: Keep a list of your team members--perhaps calling the document "opinion sharing" – and make a note of every time you sought team members' opinions. This will provide a visual guide in gauging whether you have employed proactive opinion solicitation on a frequent and distributed basis.

Other strategies: Thank team members privately and publicly when they present ideas that might go against the popularly held views of the organization. Normalize the sharing of contrasting viewpoints. Regularly communicate to team members--both in private and group settings--how their opinions specifically influenced organizational decisions, drawing a direct line between employee input and corporate output. In managerial meetings ask: How have we encouraged our teams to be opinion sharers?

Safe space to make mistakes. In Navajo culture, the custom is for rug weavers to leave little imperfections along the borders. In Japan, incorporating imperfections into art and architecture is also considered a necessary ingredient. The theory behind these "deliberate imperfections" is to remind us that we are all imperfect, impermanent, and incomplete—and, indeed, there is beauty in our imperfection.

But modern culture makes little breathing room for mistakes or failures, especially with the advent of social media and cameras on every cell phone.

The goal of the effective manager is to turn the tables and make our failures the foundation for growth. Jazz great Miles Davis phrased it this way: "If you hit a wrong note, it's the next note that you play that determines if it's good or bad." In a similar way, tennis star Billie Jean King described her mistakes on the court not as failures but as *feedback*. Each errant swing was a data point that allowed her

8. The Pentatonic Scale and the Sanctity of Safe Spaces

to recalibrate her technique. In essence, she extracted emotion out of her mistakes and instead took a scientific approach to evaluating her miscues.

In terms of practical application, managers should approach mistakes made by our teams--or us! – as feedback, not failure. Openly discuss career setbacks and the lessons learned from those setbacks. Tell stories of others who have effectively used the lessons from setbacks to promote their careers.

"...managers should approach mistakes made by our teams – or us! – as feedback not failure"

Dwelling on shortcomings can lead to a type of paralysis or even despair. But when we change our perspective and understand that imperfections are a necessary ingredient to life, we can forge ahead with confidence, knowing we can create something beautiful with the tapestries of our lives, even with the imperfections woven within.

Children's television pioneer Fred Rogers used the term "permissible regression" to describe the moments when children--for brief interludes--revert back to the activities of younger children (e.g., playing with a younger child's toy, using the language of younger children). Rogers argued that these moments of permissible regression should not be frowned upon; rather, they should be viewed as necessary points of reflection and growth in the life path of a child.

Management as Music

Just so, managers must allow their teams--and themselves--the freedom to regress professionally, recognizing that those moments of regression can be the seeds of growth.

Safe space to make independent decisions. The Oxford Dictionary defines the musical term rubato as "the temporary disregarding of strict tempo to allow an expressive quickening or slackening, usually without altering the overall pace." Effective managers employ "managerial rubato" with their teams, promoting independent experimentation within the goals and values of the organization. Healthy workplaces are laboratories of experimentation, where team members are encouraged to put on the lab coat and take calculated risks.

Effective managers highlight and tell stories of others who have taken risks to advance the overall mission of their organizations. They also model experimentation for their teams, continually sharing lessons learned from risk-taking.

Safe space to self-advocate. Team members must feel empowered to advocate for their needs (e.g., additional resources, training, promotion opportunities, or clarity about job descriptions). Just as a crucial element of child development is learning how to self-advocate for one's needs, the same is is true for our team members. To assist teams in being self-advocates:

8. The Pentatonic Scale and the Sanctity of Safe Spaces

- Tell stories of others who have successfully self-advocated for themselves, including the strategies they used.
- Be proactive in reaching out to your team, asking questions though could lead to self-advocacy. For example: What resources would make your job easier? What additional job duties would you find challenging or rewarding? Are there parts of your job description that need clarifying? What part of your job do you find draining/energizing?

Safe space to be vulnerable. The acceptance and promotion of vulnerability is perhaps the most underutilized tool of the modern-day manager.

Musicians who sing or play *a cappella* (without any accompaniment) are intensely familiar with the concept of vulnerability. Every mistake in their performance is magnified; every insecurity brought to the fore; every emotion exposed for the audience to dissect and examine. The successful musician confronts her vulnerability squarely, using the creative energy that comes from being exposed to add emotion and inspiration to her performance.

Geologist Xavier Le Pichon founded the field of plate tectonics, the theory describing how the earth's plates move and interact with each other. In a podcast, Le Pichon connected the fragility that exists in his field of geology with the fragility we find in humanity. He spoke poignantly about the earth's remarkable ability to accommodate fragility and weakness: "Fragility is the essence of men and women, and it is at the heart of humanity ... A capacity to accommodate fragility is a fundament of vital, evolving systems, whether geological or human ... *Earthquakes happen when weaknesses cannot be expressed.* And communities which don't take into account the weak points in the community, or of people who are in difficulty, tend to be communities that do not evolve."

And what is true for geology and communities is true for individuals as well. We paralyze ourselves when we bury our vulnerabilities – when we become content with the status quo and don't venture anything new. Virginia Woolf rightly observed that "if you do not tell the truth about yourself, you cannot tell it about other people."

"We paralyze ourselves when we bury our vulnerabilities"

I discovered the vitality of vulnerability when, in the aftermath of my father's death, my piano teacher gave me the most salient piece of advice I've ever received: she said don't be afraid to bang on the piano keys as an outlet of frustration, anger, and fear. The point she was trying to embed on my young heart was that there is great strength when you have the courage to expose your insecurities to the light of day. The managerial task is to give our teams that same freedom to be vulnerable.

8. The Pentatonic Scale and the Sanctity of Safe Spaces

As writer Henri Nouwen observed: "When we become aware that we do not have to escape our pains but that we can mobilize them into a common search for life, those very pains are transformed from expressions of despair into signs of hope."

By encouraging our teams (and ourselves) to expose vulnerability, we can become – as Ernest Hemingway put it – "strong at the broken places."

Ring the bells that still can ring ...
Forget your perfect offering ...
There is a crack, a crack in everything ...
That's how the light gets in.

--Musician-poet Leonard Cohen

CHAPTER 9

Management in Sonata Form

My favorite style of musical composition is the sonata. Whether it's the mystery of Beethoven's Sonata No. 14 ("Moonlight"), the lushness of Schubert's Sonata No. 21, or the transcendence of Chopin's Sonata No. 2, sonatas have always had a hold on me.

As I contemplated *why* sonatas move me as they do, the revelation came that the arch of our management lives is like a sonata. A brief music theory lesson will help provide context.

The sonata has three basic sections: exposition, development, and recapitulation. In the exposition, the main themes are introduced ("exposed") to the listener. The development is where the themes are explored in a variety of different ways (e.g., changes in key, overall mood, dynamics, and rhythm). And finally, in the recapitulation (the "homecoming" section), the main themes return, but they are elegantly transformed with a freshness due to the time they spent in the development section.

Do you see how our management and professional lives are like that? There are moments when we merely absorb the routines around us, learning lessons of how our workplaces operate and gathering tools for the journey (our "exposition"

9. Management in Sonata Form

section). Here the dominant theme is passivity. Then we begin to branch out in new and different ways, using the tools we learned earlier to forge our own unique career path (our "development" section). Finally, we reach a place of homecoming, where we synthesize the early lessons we were taught with the hard realities of our own experiences (our "recapitulation" section). This final section is our legacy to the teams we serve.

Futurist and author Alvin Toffler predicted that "(t)he illiterate of the 21st century will not be those who cannot read and write but those who cannot learn, unlearn, and relearn." Put another way: Leaders of the 21st century will be those who can think in sonata form.

Unlike Beethoven or Chopin, who had the luxury of planning out every note, we go into our management sonatas blind. We journey on without foresight of what the end will look like, and we do our composing on the fly, without any eraser to strike out mistakes. Our management careers do not always flow in a linear fashion; we sometimes find ourselves regressing, forced to relearn lessons missed the first time.

A blunt reality is that the work of a manager can be downright depressing if we only look at our current circumstances. Depression descends when our career trajectories do not progress as we envisioned. But if we and our teams can learn to view our professional lives as a

Management as Music

sonata, where lessons learned eventually transform into surprised beauty and a rich legacy, we can take heart knowing our journeys will ultimately be lusher and more transcendent than any Beethoven masterpiece.

CHAPTER 10

Startling with Silence

In the Metropolitan Museum of Art in New York City resides a 2,000-year-old "dotaku" bell from Japan that was designed to be silent. While historians still debate the purpose of these bells, it is hypothesized that their primary purpose was not to be heard but *observed*. These ancient builders understood the power and majesty of unexpected silence.

Composers, too, long ago discovered the value of unexpected silence, using the silence to create anticipation, offer a moment for reflection, or simply surprise their audiences. Mozart observed that "music is not in the notes but in the silence in between." Indeed, some of the most powerful moments in classical music history are moments of unexpected silence.

Beethoven's *Eroica* symphony, for example, builds massive momentum--full of repeating dissonant chords--and reaches a climax where the listener predicts a harmonic resolution. But instead of resolution, there is silence. Musicologists Grosvenor Cooper and Leonard Meyer called it "the loudest silence in musical literature."

Or consider how Brahm's Third and Tchaikovsky's Sixth symphonies mystically recede into silence.

Management as Music

These masterpieces would not have had the emotional impact on audiences--or the lasting influence on the landscape of music composition--if the composers had not dared to startle with silence.

There are at least five ways managers can harness the power of silence to lead their teams effectively.

First, silence is a powerful organizer of priorities. Managerial work exposes the leader to multitudes of urgent personal and institutional claims, all worthy of immediate attention. Wise decisions are rarely made in environments of distraction or stress. Thus, to evaluate and organize these competing managerial claims properly, it is helpful for mangers to allocate time on a daily basis to reflect, rejuvenate, and refocus in silence. I call these moments of reflection intentional interludes.

In a culture governed by billable hours and production indices, modern managers are not rewarded for promoting or practicing silence. Indeed, the archetypal image of a high-flying executive is one who never stops moving. But managers who regularly practice intentional interludes are able to face decisions with an attitude of reflection and not impulsivity.

Second, managers must cultivate the fine of art of *not having the last word*. Often managers explain their positions repetitively and relentlessly. We desperately seek the last word, hoping it will give us the upper hand. But the reality:

10. Startling with Silence

Once our stance on an issue has been thoroughly explained, further explanation only muddies the waters and is often counterproductive, engendering resentment and frustration. Mangers must have the fortitude to *stand in silence*, letting their words have the space to work the desired impact.

Third, silence can be a warning signal for leaders. We think of days not bombarded with endless questions as "successful." But this silence is often an indicator of lurking problems within a team. General Colin Powell observed that "(t)he day the soldiers stop bringing you their problems is the day you stopped leading them. They have either lost confidence that you can help them or concluded that you do not care. Either case is a failure of leadership." When observing extended periods of silence within your team, be intentional about checking in to ensure questions are being answered and that you are being responsive to any unresolved issues.

Fourth, silence can be used as a corrective to the danger of false urgency. Leaders can fall into the trap of framing every organizational threat or opportunity with a sense of top priority. The frequent result is that their teams treat *nothing* with urgency. Effective leaders properly prioritize organizational threats and opportunities, knowing when to create a sense of urgency and when to have a more reserved response--or even remain silent.

Lastly, our rewards as as managers will come not in moments of public recognition but in moments of silence.

Management as Music

Society views the ultimate validation of our success in very public terms--trophies polished to a shiny gleam, ornate plaques, handsomely framed certificates of achievement, verbose speeches honoring our contributions. But if leaders expect a ticker-tape parade for our efforts, we will be perpetually disappointed. It is vital that managers and their teams have healthy expectations and appreciate the reality that the ultimate reward for a job well done will come not through the noise of outward praise but the silence of inward contentment.

At Yale University's 1957 Baccalaureate service, President Dr. A. Whitney Griswold spoke eloquently of how a life of meaning is often discovered in silence. He said that professional and personal contentment "comes to us when we are alone, in quiet moments, in quiet places, when we suddenly realize that, knowing the good we have done it; knowing the beautiful, we have served it; knowing the truth, we have spoken it." The manager who internalizes these truths will have a powerful tool to ward off the cynicism so prevalent in managerial life.

Tip: Write a letter to every new manager on your team, including the quote from Dr. Griswold and highlighting how professional satisfaction is often found in silence. It might be the best advice you ever impart to them.

CHAPTER 11

The Cruciality of Counterpoint

The musical concept of counterpoint refers to two or more melodic lines (or "voices") that complement one another but act independently. The two lines can differ in rhythm and melody but are harmonically dependent (i.e., have the same tonal center). Each of the melodies is of equal importance, neither outshining the other.

Perfected by J. S. Bach, counterpoint was an important development in musical theory because it marked a divergence from monophony (music consisting of a single unaccompanied melodic line) and revealed to the world that two melodies need not be in competition but can work together toward a unified whole.

From a composer's perspective, counterpoint adds richness, variety, and energy to compositions by utilizing multiple melodies that might differ in rhythm or dynamics.[xx]

For leaders, counterpoint teaches that we must avoid pigeonholing team members, viewing them as useful for only one purpose or skill. Instead, we must always give our colleagues the freedom to voice new strategies for the organization and explore new vocational interests.

Management as Music

In July 2009, writer Chimamanda Ngozi Adichie presented a TED Talk entitled "The Danger of a Single Story," where she recounted her childhood in Nigeria, her transition to college in America, and how she became defined by a single story.

Adichie described the danger of a single story as showing "a people as one thing, as only one thing, over and over again, and that is what they become." She went on to say: "The single story creates stereotypes, and the problem with stereotypes is not that they are untrue but that they are *incomplete* ... They make one story become the only story."

Leaders must never reduce team members to a single story, imprisoning them with stereotypes that limit their full potential. Instead, effective leaders support team members in developing their own unique visions and interests (i.e., melodies) that might sound different from the organizational melody.

Methods for promoting counterpoint include:

- Encouraging team members to apply for other positions that will advance their vocational dreams, even if this might present a momentary hardship for your team.
- Relinquishing control over a project or initiative to a team member who exhibits great enthusiasm or interest in the project.

11. The Cruciality of Counterpoint

- Giving team members assignments that are outside of their normal job functions but where you think they have opportunity to grow professionally.
- Envisioning your team members in different roles, with different functions, even if the team members never change roles.

Nina Simone was the rare musician who weaved effectively between multiple musical genres. She was a classically trained pianist and could play the most difficult pieces of the classical repertoire with ease. But she became famous as a jazz musician, thrilling audiences with her inspired syncopation and improvisation.

In 1960, Simone performed the jazz standard "Love Me or Leave Me" on *The Ed Sullivan Show*. A routine affair suddenly turned extraordinary when, approximately a minute in to the performance, she transitioned seamlessly from a standard jazz format to classical, complete with an improvised counterpoint section that would have made J.S. Bach stand up and applaud.

At that moment Simone became a living embodiment of counterpoint, subtly whispering to the world that multiple melodies can coexist without disrupting harmony--that we need not be defined by a single melody, a single story. Leaders must have the courage to do the same.

CHAPTER 12

Helen Keller's "Ode to Joy"

In moments of reflective silence, musicians and managers find themselves asking similar internal questions: "Does my work make a difference? Am I influencing others? Does my audience understand or appreciate what I'm trying to accomplish? Am I bending the world toward beauty?"

On February 2, 1924, Helen Keller provided poignant answers to these lingering questions when she penned the following letter to the New York Symphony Orchestra in response to their performance of Beethoven's Symphony No. 9:

Last night, when the family was listening to your wonderful rendering of the immortal symphony someone suggested that I put my hand on the (radio) receiver and see if I could get any of the vibrations ... What was my amazement to discover that I could feel, not only the vibration, but also the impassioned rhythm, the throb and the urge of the music! The intertwined and intermingling vibrations from different instruments enchanted me. I could actually distinguish the cornets, the roll of the drums, deep toned violas and violins singing in exquisite unison ... Then all the instruments and voices together burst forth--an ocean of heavenly vibration--and died away like winds when the atom is spent, ending in a delicate shower of sweet notes.

Of course this was not "hearing," but I do know that the tones and harmonies conveyed to me moods of great beauty and majesty. I also sensed, or thought I did, the tender sounds of nature that sing into my hand-swaying reeds and winds and the murmur of streams. I have never been so enraptured before by a multitude of tone-vibrations.

As I listened, with darkness and melody, shadow and sound filling all the room, I could not help remembering that the great composer who poured forth such a flood of sweetness into the world was deaf like myself. I marveled at the power of his quenchless spirit by which out of his pain he wrought such joy for others—and there I sat, feeling with my hand the magnificent symphony which broke like a sea upon the silent shores of his soul and mine.[1]

Our world continues to reach out its hand in hopeful expectation, yearning for an inspirational note to guide the way. The lesson of Helen Keller's letter: When we send beauty into the world its vibrations can always be felt, even when not seen or heard or even understood. And that is the great hope of the musician--and the manager.

---

[1] This letter can be found in The Auricle, Vol. II, No. 6, March 1924. American Foundation for the Blind, Helen Keller Archives.

CONCLUSION

Finale: Lessons from Three Musical Vignettes

Music does not answer questions, observed Leonard Bernstein, "it provokes them; and its essential meaning is in the tension between the contradictory answers." The same is true for leadership.

The goal of these brief pages has not been to answer the endless questions posed by leadership; rather, it has been to cast a net over the music that is all around us, capturing the many facets of its emotional power, and to *provoke* questions to guide our path. What has emerged, I hope, is that the art of leadership--like music--can be reduced to two elements: technique and inspiration.

As I contemplate the perfect blend of technique and inspiration, I picture three musical vignettes: Whitney Houston's rendition of the national anthem at the 1991 Super Bowl, Aretha Franklin's performance at the 1998 Grammy Awards, and Joni Mitchell's surprise performance at the 2022 Newport Folk Festival.

Most know the general outline of Houston's 1991 Super Bowl performance: The Gulf War was 10 days old, anxieties were high, and the nation yearned for a galvanizing moment of patriotic excitement. Houston, dressed in a tracksuit and headband, responded by offering a rendition that has

Finale: Lessons from Three Musical Vignettes

become the gold standard for all who have followed. Less known is the backstory of how Houston's version came to be. It is this backstory that offers lessons for managers.

When originally approached to sing the anthem, Houston told her music director, Rickey Minor, that she wanted to sing a non-traditional rendition (much like Marvin Gaye's performance at the 1983 NBA All Star game). With that mandate as a guide, Houston and arranger John Clayton, Jr., created a version that challenged the expectation of the audience in at least four ways.

First, they added a beat to each measure (going from 3/4 to 4/4 time). This allowed Houston more opportunity within each measure to nurture and give nuance to each note. Second, they made liberal use of reharmonization (for example, using a IV chord when the listener expected a I chord). This gave the piece a jazz and gospel feel without altering the overall melody. Third, they made a dramatic change in dynamics (going from a strong *forte* to *piano*) at the second section ("Whose broad stripes ...") This contrast allowed the audience a chance to catch its breath, reflect, and regroup before the climatic closing section. Finally, they made the word "free" (as opposed to the final word "brave") the musical climax. Here Houston altered the melody by continuing upward. When describing this ascent on the word "free," writer Clinque Henderson observed that it was if the notes were "simply hiding in the air waiting to be

Management as Music

found and, once Houston had seen and sung them, they would never be hidden again."

After hearing a demo of Houston's version, executives from the NFL and CBS pushed back, fearing a backlash from the audience. They asked her to sing another arrangement. Even the orchestra that played the accompaniment questioned the rhythmic and harmonic alterations to one of the most recognizable songs in the world. No one would have begrudged Houston for relenting and reverting to a familiar arrangement. She was at the height of her popularity, with absolutely nothing to gain by challenging the status quo. But Houston did not waiver; she had the fortitude to fail.

Fast forward to 1998. Aretha Franklin was slated to make a brief performance at the Grammys, singing one of her standards. Also to perform was legendary operatic tenor Luciano Pavarotti, who was receiving a Lifetime Achieve Award. Pavarotti was to sing his signature piece, "Nessun Dorma" from Puccini's *Turnadot*. The aria was to be the highlight of the entire broadcast. But less than an hour before he was set to take stage, Pavarotti informed the producers that a nasty throat infection would keep him on the sidelines.

Naturally, the producers panicked. How do you replace the most famous operatic singer in the world on a moment's notice? Do you simply scrap the number altogether? Or get

Finale: Lessons from Three Musical Vignettes

another performer to sing one of their own hits? Who would be willing to sing *anything* with no time to prepare?

The lead producer suddenly remembered that Franklin previously sang a modified version of "Nessun Dorma" at a benefit concert. She rushed to Franklin's dressing room and asked if there was any possibility that she could step in and sing. Franklin asked for a recording of the dress performance done earlier in the day. After hearing the recording, she simply stated: "Yeah, I can do that."

Franklin had little to gain in accepting this last-minute request. For starters, she was tackling the signature song of an operatic legend. Add to that: she was not an operatic singer; the song was in Italian; she was a mezzo-soprano and not a tenor (and she had to sing it in the tenor range); she had no time to rehearse with the orchestra; and she had never sung the version of the song before. Not to mention she had to do it all in front of an audience of millions!

You have probably already predicted the result. Franklin was the hit of the night, and her performance has been ranked as the number one Grammy moment ever.

Now turn to July of 2022. 78-year old Joni Mitchell gingerly took the stage at the Newport Folk Festival, a place she had become famous 55 years earlier, popularizing such classics as "The Circle Game." Mitchell's presence was a surprise, as she had been plagued by health problems for years, including a 2015 brain aneurysm that required her to relearn how to sing. It was her first full-length public concert in over 20 years, and mobility problems required her to sit for the entire performance. The force behind Mitchell's return was singer Brandi Carlile, who spent years working to preserve and promote Mitchell's legacy, especially among younger performers.

As Mitchell sang her classic "Both Sides Now," the sound was completely different from her twenty-year-old self who had written the song and captivated a generation. She was now an alto, not a soprano, and her breathing capacity was severely limited, restricting her ability to sing long phrases. Instead of sticking to her original arrangement, she lowered the key, strategically altered the melody, changed the phrasing, utilized the other musicians to provide her additional harmonic support, and had her friend Brandi Carlile join her when she knew her voice lacked the range to hit the required high notes. The performance was rightly lauded as a master class of musical excellence, defying the audience's expectations with top-shelf creativity that also honored the original composition.

What lessons do these three vignettes offer leaders seeking to compose melodies with elevated technique and inspiration?

Never stop learning. Franklin, Houston, and Mitchell constantly honed their skills and were therefore well positioned to take advantage of the unique opportunities

Finale: Lessons from Three Musical Vignettes

presented to them. Transformative leadership is a *path to pursue*, not a destination to reach.

Adapt, adapt, adapt. All three artists did a thorough self-assessment of their abilities and the vision they wanted to create, strategically adapting their performances to achieve maximum impact. Effective leadership requires evolution, which often means abandoning strategies that worked in the past.

Do not be afraid to take risks. All three had the confidence in themselves to risk failure. Meaningful leadership never arises from timidity. There is no tiptoeing toward greatness.

We all need supporters. All three needed collaborators and supporters to make their special moments materialize. Great leadership only emerges in community and collaboration with others.

Be true to yourself. All three felt free to break away from old formulas and make each song their own. Consequential leadership is always authentic, never derivative.

*****

Managers walk daily into the arena called leading others. The supporting cast is assembled, the onlooking crowd is primed, expectations are high, and we nervously approach the microphone.

Management as Music

The choice: Will we stick to a familiar arrangement, relying on old metaphors to guide the way? Or will we harness the lessons of music and have the courage to alter our rhythms, harmonies, and melodies, thereby risking failure for something great?

An anxious world awaits our song.

―――――――――――――――

AFTERWORD

Coda: A Note on Unfinished Symphonies

Franz Schubert's Symphony No. 8 has been labeled the "Unfinished Symphony" because he only completed two movements before his death. Music enthusiasts have long mourned that one of the 19th century's most creative musical talents died before giving the world one more transforming work of art. On the 100th anniversary of Schubert's death, Columbia Records even held a competition for composers to submit their best completions to Schubert's unfinished work.

Instead of viewing Schubert's unfinished symphony as a tragedy, I submit that we should look upon it with a sense of hope. Consider that some of the most heroic figures of modern history have been viewed as failures in their lifetime (Abraham Lincoln, Gandhi, and Martin Luther King, Jr., just to name a few). It was only *after* death that their visions were more fully realized and their impacts more fully appreciated. They became heroes not because of goals achieved during their lifetimes; they became heroes because they never stopped fighting for the future they had the courage to envision.

Those who flinch in the prospect of failure usually are absorbed silently into the status quo. But those who look

Management as Music

failure in the eye gain the confidence to envision a new and better future.

The bottom line: We will never finish our management symphonies. Even if our pens keep composing to our final breath, there will be goals not accomplished, strategies unfinished, skills not refined, and relationships not fully nourished.

The question is not whether we will complete our symphonies. The question is whether we keep composing until the very end, trusting that our melodies will continue to inspire the lives of others, even when our final earthly notes have faded into mystic silence.

APPENDIX: CASE STUDIES IN MANAGERIAL STORYTELLING

The following are examples of communications I sent my team over a span of several years.

I hesitated to include examples of my own team communication, as these messages were created at a particular moment in time, under unique workplace stresses, with a particular purpose--all of which would be unfamiliar to the reader. But my hope is that these examples provide a template for how storytelling can be a powerful promoter of organizational objectives.

*****

1. The Power of Encouragement

At the age of nine, John O'Leary suffered third-degree burns on 100 percent of his body and was given a 1% chance of survival. When O'Leary laid in the hospital—strapped to his bed, eyes swollen shut, a tracheotomy lodged in his throat—one of his first visitors was legendary St. Louis Cardinals broadcaster Jack Buck. O'Leary lived in St. Louis, and his obsession was the Cardinals. O'Leary immediately recognized Buck's booming voice at the bedside: "Kid, wake up! You are going to live! You are going to survive and keep fighting!"

Management as Music

Buck's visits continued like clockwork during O'Leary's long hospital stay. But Buck didn't stop there. When O'Leary had to relearn how to write (since his hands were deformed in the fire), Buck sent O'Leary a signed baseball from O'Leary's favorite player. The ball had a note attached: "Kid, if you want a second baseball, all you have to do is sign a thank-you letter to the man who sent the first one." With assistance from his parents, O'Leary wrote that first thank-you note. And the signed balls continued. By the end of 1987, Buck sent O'Leary 60 signed balls. O'Leary described the experience this way: "Sixty baseballs from a very busy guy teaching a little nobody in St. Louis how to write."

But the story doesn't end there. Buck continued to keep in touch with O'Leary. When O'Leary graduated from Saint Louis University, Buck presented him with the crystal baseball the broadcaster received when he was inducted into the Baseball Hall of Fame. One more life-affirming act of kindness.

We all need affirming voices like Jack Buck in our lives. Voices that support us through the good and bad. Voices that never stop proclaiming our worth and value, even when we don't feel valuable at all. Being an affirming voice is not easy work—it takes dedication and persistence. But it's the least we can do for those who have been beacons of affirmation in our own lives.

*****

2. The Lesson of a Healed Femur

A student once asked the famed anthropologist Margaret Mead what she considered the first harbinger of civilization. Mead thought a moment and answered: "A healed femur."

Why would Mead answer that way? Other human achievements—the wheel, pottery, agricultural advancements, harnessing fire—are often seen as the spearhead of civilization. She defended her answer this way: In the wild, animals with broken femurs are left for dead, as they have no way to protect themselves or gather food. A healed femur, Mead explained, shows that someone looked after the safety and health of the injured person. Put even more simply, a healed femur represents *compassion*. And that compassion translates into cooperation and ultimately civilization.

If Mead is right that compassion is the spearhead of civilization—and I think she *is* right—then it only makes sense for our communities to leverage that compassion in new and creative ways, especially in times of stress and anxiety. We currently live in some pretty stressful and anxious times. So, what does compassion look like in a time of COVID-19 and social distancing?

It looks like the story of NBA players, like Zion Williamson, donating money to pay arena employees who would lose money due to the suspension of the NBA season.

Management as Music

It looks like the story of restaurants, closed by the COVID outbreak, donating excess food to local food banks.

It looks like the story of two young cellists who played a spontaneous concert outside of the house of an elderly, quarantined neighbor.

I truly believe our future is as bright and boundless as our ability to find compassionate outlets for our anxieties. Compassion is the key to combating our anxieties.

*****

3. Lessons from Hawthorne's "The Great Stone Face"

My mother, who was a high school English teacher, instilled in me a love for mid-nineteenth century American literature (to be honest, I don't know if this was a blessing or a curse!) In particular, the short stories of that era have always appealed to me. One such example is Nathaniel Hawthorne's "The Great Stone Face."

The protagonist of the story is Ernest, who lived in a valley nestled between several large mountains. Etched into one of the mountain facades was a formation resembling the image of a wise, benevolent face (the "Great Stone Face"). The local legend was that a person whose appearance matched the Great Stone Face would one day return to the

Appendix: Case Studies in Managerial Storytelling

valley and be "the greatest and noblest personage of his time."

Throughout Ernest's life, several contenders emerged as potential fulfillments of the prophecy, including a wealthy merchant, a respected politician, an accomplished writer, and a revered general. But each was rejected as not fully capturing the wisdom and benevolence of the Great Stone Face. As these great pretenders came and went, Ernest quietly grew old contemplating the lessons of the mysterious mountain image. He would often share his thoughts with friends and neighbors. And on one such occasion, when he went at sunset to discourse with a gathering of the villagers, "his words had power … and depth because they harmonized with the life which he had always lived … They were the words of life, because a life of good deeds and love was melted into them." As he spoke, "the face of Ernest assumed a grandeur of expression, so inbred with benevolence" that a wise poet stood up and proclaimed: "Behold! Behold! Ernest has himself the likeness of the Great Stone Face!"

But Ernest did not accept the title. No, "having finished what he had to say, (he) took the poet's arm, and walked slowly homeward, still hoping that some wiser and better man than himself would by and by appear…"

For me, three lessons emerge from Hawthorne's brief tale.

Lessons from the preparation of Ernest. Ernest spent a lifetime of reflection and study, but it was not until his *final act* that the results of his efforts appeared to pay off. To be sure, Ernest must have despaired when his search for the Great Stone Face turned up empty again and again, but he continued his search nonetheless. The lesson? A life of significance is often subterranean, operating for years in unseen preparation until one day the network of roots that have patiently formed break through to splendid daylight.

Lessons from the reaction of Ernest. Even after villagers declared him to be the Great Stone Face, Ernest kept his humility and indicated there was still work to be done. Here we learn the importance of persistence and staying modest when cultivating a life of meaning. Often humility is the most effective vessel we have to transfer our compassion and care to others.

Lessons from the reaction of the villagers. It was not until Ernest was old that the villagers vocalized any recognition for his life. Year after year Ernest did the mundane work of contemplating, encouraging, and providing wisdom to his fellow villagers, all without any apparent celebration of his efforts. The lesson? Often in life they'll be no applause for our hard work. But while words of appreciation may never flow our way, we can take heart in knowing our acts of humility and kindness are still performing their transformative work behind the scenes.

Appendix: Case Studies in Managerial Storytelling

Let us never forget that the preparations we make along the way are important; that our work is never complete until the very end; and that our actions have a lasting impact on others, even if they appear to go unnoticed.

*****

4. What Will We Leave Behind? (Lessons from "Cleopatra's Needle")

In 1877, archaeologists discovered "Cleopatra's Needle," a granite obelisk hidden deep in the sands of Egypt. Once the labyrinth of hieroglyphics on its facade were deciphered, the Needle told the story of a civilization long forgotten. Plans were made to move the obelisk to the heart of a London as a gift to the British people. But as preparations were being made to make the move, the question arose: What if, 3,000 years later, some future generation unearthed the obelisk again? What representation of the current civilization should be transmitted to the future? The decision was made to place a time capsule at the base of the Needle. Into the capsule went representative reflections of contemporary life: a set of coins; weights and measures; children's toys; clothing.

As I reflect on the objects that were selected to represent 19th century life, it strikes me how the objects didn't speak to the *will* of the people. No mention of bravery, overcoming adversity, or ingenuity. No mention of heroism or creativity.

What will we leave in our time capsule to tell the story of the current COVID-19 period? Let us select something that proclaims *hope*...

Like a homemade mask, for the countless ways creativity bloomed; or a stethoscope, representing the bravery and heroism of medical professionals; or a graduation cap, symbolizing the resilience of students who had their plans turned upside down in an instant; or a computer mouse, reflecting our pivot to new ways of communicating, learning, and working.

For what really survives the ages—more than coins, or toys, or clothes—is the *hope* of a people. May that be our everlasting gift to the future.

*****

5. Hope from the Year of the Locust

Future success is sometimes born out of crisis.

In 1874, millions of locusts descended on the Great Plains. Families watched helplessly as armies of locusts devoured whole crops, wool off sheep, paint off wagons, even quilts that had been carefully draped over vegetable gardens. They feasted and feasted until there was nothing left. One report

Appendix: Case Studies in Managerial Storytelling

released in 1874 suggested that just one family in 10 had enough provisions to last the coming winter. The locust plague constituted the worst natural disaster in the country's history.

Imagine how those farmers must have felt, standing at the edge of the prairie, surveying the destruction of their livelihoods. These families worked for months preparing and cultivating their crops. And then, in an instant, everything was gone.

Amid COVID-19, we may be feeling a little like those farmers—plans dashed, preparations shattered, dreams deferred. But was it all for naught? Were our preparations wasted? Will anything good come out of this pandemic?

There is hope from the aftermath of the year of the locust. The millions of locusts who died fertilized the soil that was left behind. The result? Many farmers found the years *after* the locusts descended to be their best harvests. May the same be true for us. May the work we do now—during this current crisis—sow the seeds of our future success.

*****

6. Crisis as Catalyst for Creative Giving (Lessons from Candy Land)

Crisis can be the catalyst for creative giving.

Management as Music

I was fascinated to read in the July 2019 issue of *The Atlantic* that the popular board game Candy Land was created inside a polio ward during the polio epidemic of the 1940's and 50's. I filed the article away in a filing cabinet, not knowing that it would have added meaning some eight months later.

Candy Land's inventor, Eleanor Abbott, was a teacher recovering from polio. She created the game for her fellow quarantined patients (most of them children) as a way of giving them a liberating sense of freedom of mobility midst their confinement. Every element of the game's simple design was carefully crafted to give hope for those playing, to transport them to a world where anything was possible. If you look closely at the original game board you'll even see a boy with a leg brace, a simple act intended to bond with the countless children who would have lifelong residual effects from their bouts with polio. Milton Bradley was quick to buy the game from Abbott, and it became one of the best-selling board games of all time.

During the current pandemic, people are finding countless, creative ways to use their confinement to inspire others. Here is a sampling:

(1) Cellist Yo-Yo Ma records daily inspirational musical selections and posts them on Facebook;

Appendix:: Case Studies in Managerial Storytelling

(2) Many are organizing car "parades" to celebrate the birthdays of their quarantined friends;

(3) Actor John Krasinski records a daily video called "Some Good News" where he focuses on positive, inspirational stories;

(4) Broadway singer Brian Stokes Mitchell sings from his Upper West Side apartment window every evening to thank first responders;

(5) In my hometown, the Air Force flew planes over local hospitals to show support for healthcare workers.

How will we deploy our unique talents to inspire others during the COVID-19 crisis?

*****

7. The Quality Quest in a Time of Crisis

Crisis can be the catalyst for a renewed focus on quality.

Japan's economy was in shambles following World War II. Gen. Douglas MacArthur commissioned several business and management leaders to assist Japan with the daunting task of rebuilding its beleaguered manufacturing sector. Among this select team was Dr. W. E. Deming, an industrial statistician who specialized in business management. Deming advocated to Japanese business leaders a revolutionary management style, which he later outlined in the book *Out of the Crisis*.

At the heart of Deming model was a focus on three ideas: quality, improvement, and process. More specifically, businesses should "create constancy of purpose toward improvement of product and service" (quality); "improve constantly and forever the system of production and service" (process); "institute a vigorous program of education and self-improvement" (improvement); "institute training on the job" (improvement); and "break down barriers between departments ... to foresee problems of production" (quality and process). Instead of focusing exclusively on the end product, Deming argued that businesses should focus on the *processes* that resulted in the end product and continuously ensure those processes had the mark of quality. Put even more simply, if the manufacturing processes were high quality, the results would take care of themselves.

Japanese businesses eventually adopted Deming's model, and the result was decades of unprecedented manufacturing grow.

In response to the economic recession of the late 1970s and early 1980s, U.S. companies slowly began to implement the Deming model as well. Many attribute the U.S's manufacturing resurgence in the late 1980s and 1990s to the wide-scale adoption of Deming's focus on quality, improvement, and process.

My view is that the Deming model can be applied not only in the business world but to our personal lives as well. Sometimes we focus so narrowly on our end destination that we fail to appreciate the little steps it takes to get there.

To be sure, our hectic everyday schedules barely give us time to take a breath, much less ask probing questions like: Are our processes helping or hindering us? Are there more efficient ways to perform this task? Are our daily routines benefiting our overall goals?

But maybe this time of quarantine is an ideal opportunity for us to slow down and evaluate the daily rhythms (processes) that animate our lives.

*****

8. Lessons from *Rocketman*

I recently saw *Rocketman*, the biographical movie about Elton John. As I watched the brilliantly told story of how Elton overcame numerous obstacles to become one of the most successful pop stars ever, several lessons—along with the beautiful melodies!—lingered with me.

First, Elton recognized his weaknesses. He quickly realized that, while composing melodies came easily to him, writing

Management as Music

lyrics was a stumbling block. He posted an advertisement in the newspaper for a lyricist, and Bernie Taupin quickly responded. The rest is music history. Often, we put on blinders and fail to see we don't have all the answers. But by reaching out to others who complement our own talents, we can grow professionally and personally, becoming the best versions of ourselves.

Second, Elton was constantly evolving. He never confined himself to a particular style, and he always honed his craft. The variety of his songs is simply astounding. And the fact that he was able to adapt and top the charts in five different decades is unparalleled. The lesson for us? So often we take the easy path and stick to the patterns and routines that have worked for us in the past. But the key to surviving and thriving over the long haul is adapting. As the brilliant basketball coach John Wooden put it: "The key to stability is flexibility."

Lastly, Elton had those who nurtured his talents. While his parents were generally not supportive of his budding musical ambitions, his grandmother was a constant beacon of encouragement. And later, lyricist Bernie Taupin was a rock of support through Elton's personal and professional travails. The takeaway here is that even the most innately talented among us need encouragers for us to reach our full potential.

While the talents of Elton John come along only once a generation, the lessons from his success apply to us all.

Appendix:: Case Studies in Managerial Storytelling

*****

9. The Lesson of Jim Thorpe's Shoes

Jim Thorpe is widely considered one of the best—and most versatile—athletes of the 20th century, excelling in track and field, baseball, and football. I have a picture of him in my office at home. His picture is in my office not because of his athletic accomplishments but rather because of what happened at the 1912 Olympics in Stockholm, Sweden.

In the moments before he was set to compete, someone stole Thorpe's shoes. Imagine—right before the biggest moment of your life, someone purposely tries to derail your dreams.

How did he react? Did he withdraw from the race in disgust? Did he wallow in self-pity? No, he went to a trash bin and found two shoes that someone had tossed away. They were in terrible condition and not even his size. In fact, each shoe was a different size, so he had to wear extra socks on one foot! But he went on to win two Gold medals with those ill-fitting shoes.

The lesson of Jim Thorpe's shoes is that life throws us all circumstances that are not fair. No one escapes life without adversity. The important thing is that we search for opportunities in those adversities. Sometimes an adversity can be the seed of something great.

Management as Music

*****

10. The Antidote to Hardship is Relationships

During the Civil War, the U.S. Patent Office was used as an infirmary for wounded and dying Union soldiers. They were treated between the shelves storing the country's cutting-edge inventions. The irony of this image, for me, is that the most advanced technology of that age couldn't prevent the horror of war. The soldiers could only stare at the novelties carefully stored on the shelves, for none of the inventions could provide any aid. Fast forward 155 years. Despite remarkable advances in medical care, we still cannot eliminate the tiniest of enemies—a microscopic virus.

If the sweep of human history has taught us anything it's that technological advances will never fully shield us from hardship. So how should we prepare for (and respond to) the inevitable arrival of adversity? I think Harvard's "Happiness Study" points us in the right direction.

Harvard researchers toiled for over 75 years to produce the monumental Grant and Glueck studies (dubbed the "Happiness Study"). This research tracked the well-being (both physical and mental) of two groups: 456 poor men growing up in disadvantaged neighbors in Boston from 1939 to 2014 (the Grant Study) and 268 graduates from Harvard's classes of 1939-1944 (the Glueck study). (The surviving participants are still being followed!) Harvard researcher Robert Waldinger summarized the findings this

Appendix: Case Studies in Managerial Storytelling

way: "The clearest message that we get from this 75-year study is this: Good relationships keep us happier and healthier. Period... (And) it's not just the number of friends you have...It's the quality of your close relationships that matter." Relationships outweighed all other factors, including wealth, social status, and occupational status.

The takeaway from all this? The act of relationship building is important stuff. These deepened bonds provide us fuel for the journey and a scaffolding of support when hardships come. Let us use this time of quarantine to find creative ways to cultivate those relationships that nourish us the most.

*****

11. Wind the Clock

One of my favorite authors is E .B. White (of *Charlotte's Web* fame). In 1973, White responded this way to a writer who expressed despair about the future:

"Sailors have an expression about the weather: they say, the weather is a great bluffer. I guess the same is true of our human society—things can look dark, then a break shows in the clouds, and all is changed, sometimes rather suddenly ... (A)s a people we harbor seeds of goodness that have lain for a long time waiting to sprout when the conditions are right ... Hang on to your hat. Hang on to

Management as Music

your hope. ***And wind the clock, for tomorrow is another day.***"

I think White's optimism and advice to "wind the clock" is spot on. But how do we put that optimism into action? How do we make it a daily reality? When I contemplate the answer to that question, I think of my father-in-law. At age nine, he was severely burned in an accident. He spent months in the hospital and in rehabilitation, underwent 58 surgeries, and missed a year of school. The experience was so traumatic that, for years to come, he could not step foot in a hospital room.

But my father-in-law decided to transform a tragedy into a vessel for encouraging others. He is now a burn volunteer, counseling and comforting other burn survivors as they recover physically and emotionally.

Living right outside of New Orleans, my in-laws make it to St. Charles Avenue every Mardi Gras day. My father-in-law was at the parade route again this morning, watching the oversized floats pass under the canopy of old oaks lining the crowded sidewalk. How grateful I am for this encourager—this man who winds the clock every day.

*****

12. A Reflection on Optimism

I remember my father every time I look at a tube of toothpaste.

My dad was diagnosed with cancer in his thirties, and his condition ebbed and flowed for several years. He lived with the ominous reality that this condition could deteriorate very quickly or that he could survive for several more years. What a paradox to live with!

Years after my dad finally succumbed to the disease, a friend passed along a story that always stuck with me. He said my dad once made the statement that "I never know what size of toothpaste to buy at the grocery store. Do I buy the large pack of toothpaste, knowing that there is the possibility I will never use it? Or do I simply settle for something smaller?" What struck me--and my friend--about the story was that every day my dad had to make the decision whether to be optimistic or pessimistic about his terminal medical condition. And my dad always chose to be optimistic... He always bought the large pack of toothpaste.

In the months before his death, he passed along to me a quote that I think epitomizes his philosophy of optimism: "The longer I live, the more I realize the impact of attitude on life. Attitude, to me, is more important than facts. It is more important than the past, than education, than money, than circumstances, than failures, than successes, than what other people think or say or do. (W)e have a choice every day regarding the attitude we will embrace for that day. We cannot change our past. We cannot change the fact that people will act in a certain way. We cannot change the inevitable. The only thing we can do is play on the one string we have, and that is our attitude. I am convinced that life is 10% what happens to me and 90% how I react to it. And so it is with you. We are in charge of our attitudes."

Yes, I remember my father every time I look at a tube of toothpaste. And his optimism inspires me still.

*****

13. My Three Pillars of Leadership

Studies have shown that there is no "cookie cutter" template for leadership (as much as some self-help gurus would tell us differently!) To be sure, there are certain qualities that leaders should evoke in others—e.g., trust, loyalty, respect—but how you *get there* is where the mystery of leadership comes into play. Above all, research shows that leaders must be authentic to themselves in crafting a style that is meaningful and effective.

At the heart of my philosophy of leadership are three pillars—1) gratitude, 2) servanthood, and 3) encouragement.

Appendix: Case Studies in Managerial Storytelling

Gratitude—Max Weber taught us that bureaucracy can create efficiencies, but experience has also shown it can result in those within the bureaucracy feeling insignificant. In an organization our size, necessity demands that certain processes must be systematized so that our office runs smoothly. But my overriding goal has been to show each of you gratitude for the vital part you play in the success of the office. I did not always succeed in that effort, but please know I went to work every day seeking ways to make you feel valued. I have a gratitude journal by my desk, and you each made an appearance in that journal.

Servanthood—Leaders must have servant hearts. The concept of servant leadership was first introduced by Robert K. Greenleaf in his 1970 essay "The Servant as Leader." His main point was that good leaders must first become good servants. Here's a quote from that essay: "The servant-leader is servant first ... It begins with the natural feeling that one wants to serve, to serve first. Then conscious choice brings one to aspire to lead ... The servant-leader shares power, puts the needs of others first and helps people develop and perform as highly as possible." Again, sometimes I failed miserably at this, but my heart was always oriented to finding ways—even if they were just small ways!—to make your jobs easier.

Encouragement—One of my mentors wrote: "(L)ife is a set of relationships, an 'exchange of value' with everyone we meet, and there are only three bottom lines resulting from these transactions: taking, keeping, and giving. The issue is fairly simple: does the world exist to bless me, or do I exist to bless the world? Do I live to see how much I can get from others, or do I live to see how much I can give to others?" The bottom line of life really is that simple. We can encourage others by giving of our time, attention, and experience—or we can keep those precious gifts to ourselves.

Writer C. S. Lewis said it best: "The task of the modern educator is not to cut down jungles but to irrigate deserts."

I hope that whatever deposit from my leadership remains with you will flourish in new and creative ways as the years go by. I encourage each of you to develop your own way of leading that is authentic to who you are—because we are *all* leaders, regardless of the title behind our name.

*****

14. Two Ways to Respond in Crisis

There are two ways to respond in crisis: isolation (passive retreat) or generosity (active giving). These two models are exemplified in the public response during two crises of the 20th century—the 1918 influenza pandemic and the Great Depression.

Appendix: Case Studies in Managerial Storytelling

The 1918 Pandemic. I read an interesting article in *The Atlantic* magazine recently about how, in the aftermath of the 1918 influenza pandemic, social bonds were deeply frayed. Like now, the 1918 pandemic resulted in Americans being quarantined and ceasing normal social activity. But once life returned to normal, many became more distrusting of others. They never fully integrated back into society. It was though they had forgotten how to live in community together. Obviously, this was not universally the case, but personal accounts detailed by historians in the years after the pandemic make it clear many communities took years to see renewed social connections emerge.

The Great Depression. During (and in the wake of) the Great Depression, the public response was vastly different. A sense of unity developed, resulting in an explosion of generosity. Citizens rallied to help one another in countless, creative ways. Neighbors gave food to neighbors. Community ("Relief") gardens bloomed in every town. Civic organizations emerged to assist those who had lost everything. Business leaders formed foundations to help rebuild the social fabric that had been torn by the economic calamity. Of course, not every Scrooge had a metamorphosis, but the tenor of the time was one of giving.

How will we respond to the Great Pandemic of 2020? Will we remain in our social cocoons even after it is safe to emerge? Or will we respond with an energetic generosity to each other? I'm confident we will respond with generosity.

Management as Music

But the choice is up to each of us. Our future is as bright and boundless as our ability to show radical generosity to our neighbors.

NOTES

[i] Chanda, M.L., & Levitin, D. (2013). The neurochemistry of music. *Trends in Cognitive Studies, 17*(4), 179-193.

[ii] Emerson, S., Gouzousasis P., & Guhn, M. (2020). A population-level analysis of associations between school music participation and academic achievement. *Journal of Educational Psychology, 112*(2), 308-328.

[iii] Arora, R., Chandrasekar, S., Loomba, R., Molnar, J., & Shah, P. 2012). Effects of music on systolic blood pressure, diastolic blood pressure, and heart rate: a meta-analysis. *Indian Heart Journal, 64*(3), 309-313.

[iv] King, J., Jones, K., Goldberg, E., Rollins, M., MacNamee, K., Moffit, C., Naidu, S., Ferguson, M., Garcia-Leavitt, E., Amaro, J., Breitenbach, K., Watson, J., Gurgel, R., Anderson, J., & Foster, N. (2018). Increased functional connectivity after listening to favored music in adults with Alzheimer dementia. *The Journal Of Prevention of Alzheimer's Disease*, 1–7.

[v] For a comprehensive treatment of this topic, see Lippman, E. (1964). *Musical Thought in Ancient Greece.* Columbia University Press.

[vi] Alluri, V., Toiviainen, P., Jääskeläinen, I. P., Glerean, E., Sams, M., & Brattico, E. (2012). Large-scale brain networks emerge from dynamic processing of musical timbre, key and rhythm. *NeuroImage, 59*(4), 3677–3689.

[vii] Bernstein, Leonard (1976). *The Unanswered Question: Six Talks at Harvard.* Volume 33 of Charles Eliot Norton Lectures. Harvard University Press.

[viii] Montagu, J. (2017). How music and instruments began: A brief overview of the origin and entire development of music, from its earliest stages. *Frontiers in Sociology, 2.*

[ix] From the keynote address given at the 2021 ACDA National Conference.

[x] This poem is in the public domain.

[xi] Price, R. (1989). *A Common Room, Essays 1954–1987* (First Edition). Scribner Paper Fiction.

[xii] Pérez, P., Madsen, J., Banellis, L., Türker, B., Raimondo, F., Perlbarg, V., Valente, M., Niérat, M. C., Puybasset, L., Naccache, L., Similowski, T., Cruse, D., Parra, L. C., & Sitt, J. D. (2021). Conscious processing of narrative stimuli ynchronizes heart rate between individuals. *Cell Reports, 36* (11), 109692.

Notes

[xiii] Tkachenko, O., Quast, L., Song, W., & Jang, S. (2020). Courage in the workplace: The effects of organiztional level and gender on the relationship between behavioral courage and job performance. *Journal of Management & Organization, 26*(5), 899-915.

[xiv] Capps, K. (2017, December 13). How to Build an Orchestra From Broken Instruments. *The Atlantic*.

[xv] Chesterton, G. K. (1908). *The Man Who Was Thursday* (First ed.). J.W. Arrowsmith.

[xvi] Gino, F., & Staats, B. (2015, October 19). *Why Organizations Don't Learn.* Harvard Business Review. https://hbr.org/2015/11/why-organizations-dont-learn

[xvii] *The Harvard Concise Dictionary of Music* defines dissonant intervals "as having an instability that requires resolution to a consonance."

[xviii] Solomon, A. (2012). *Far From the Tree: Parents, Children and the Search for Identity* (1st ed.). Scribner.

[xix] Amabile, T & Kramer, S. (2011, May). *The Power of Small Wins.* Harvard Business Review. https://hbr.org/2011/05/the-power-of-small-wins

Made in the USA
Las Vegas, NV
08 April 2025